THE DAY GOD SAW ME AS BLACK

•

D. DANYELLE THOMAS

THE DAY GOD SAW ME AS BLACK

The Journey to Liberated Faith

FOREWORD BY AUNJANUE ELLIS-TAYLOR

Library of Congress Cataloging-in-Publication Data Available Upon Request
ISBN 978-1-955905-53-4 (HC)
ISBN 978-1-955905-54-1 (eBook)

Design by Neuwirth & Associates, Inc.
Printed in the United States of America
Distributed by Simon & Schuster
First edition
10 9 8 7 6 5 4 3 2 1

For my Bonus Parents, Chevonna & Rick, who have always loved me beyond measure.

My Daddy, Rev. Danny Thomas Sr. (ibaye), whose pride and joy continues to breathe strength into me.

For my Sisi & Soulmie, Valerie, with all my love.

& especially for Mama, Kim. May every praise I ever receive reflect that the best of me is always because of you.

CONTENTS

THE DAY GOD SAW ME AS BLACK

•

Foreword

I FIRST SAW MYSELF THROUGH the refracting irises of blue eyes. The eyes of a pink-hued man with sinewed arms reached out in an embrace that never seemed to reach me. Rev. Varnado placed his hands on my head and heart as he plunged my eight-year-old body with Kool-Aid red socks into cold water at the pierced feet of the Blue-Eyed Man while The Mothers led the congregation in "Take Me to the Water." Every Sunday, I was warned my trespasses would turn that baptismal water to blistering flame. So I concealed myself—the little girl who knew at eight that I loved other girls. The little girl who knew that I would never submit to any man. The girl who was told not to question God. But I had as many questions as there are plaits on the heads of the little Black girls at New Home Missionary Baptist Church in McComb, Mississippi.

A child seeing themselves for the first time is definitive. If the seeing is done through reflection, the returning image is perhaps "I am my mother's child." When seeing is done through refraction, the image returns misshapen. Bent. Askew. The image returned from the Blue-Eyed Man told me what I was not. I was not pink-hued. I was not white. I didn't have blue eyes or straight hair. In my *seeing*, the Blue-Eyed Man looked like the terrorists who necklaced Black people with sisal rope. The Mothers of the church cried, moaned, laughed, and *danced* for the Blue-Eyed Man. I would soon join them in fearful surrender.

"Do you know him?" they'd ask. "*Do you know Him?* His name is Jesus. *Tarry* there. *Call* on His name! *Jesus*, Jesus!" Blue-Eyed Jesus left me bereft, but these Mothers, these Southern Black Church Women were my earthen *cloud of witnesses*. I was clay in their praying hands. These Mothers—Sister Juanita, Sister Daisy, the Sisters Varnado, Vertis, and Ella—were led in purpose and power by my grandmother, Sister Myrtis Taylor. They all had cracked tile impressions on their Hanes stockinged knees. They shaped me, molded me, made me. What is good in me is good because of their great witness and their great kiln.

I came to live with my grandmother when I was three, and she was in her sixties—tethered together by abandonment. Hers was marked by her pastor-husband who wasn't supposed to die of a heart attack on a routine revival trip to California. Mine by her daughter, my mother, whom I barely knew but still loved deeply. Loving me in the way she knew best, she held my walnut-size hand and took me to church. By the time I was eighteen, I was there at least four days of the seven-day week. New Home was my second home. I knew it intimately, how it felt, its textures. The hardness of its pews. The cold of the floor. The soft velvet on the bed of the offering plate. I knew its smells of sweated nylons and cooked greens. The echoing music from the organ of the cobalt-haired, heavy-footed Sister Alma Varnado, which was not so much song as a seawall of sound. I was made and unmade there. How is this both? How am I broken by what has held me together? How am I bolted together by what has torn me apart?

• • •

Carolyn, the first girl I loved, lived *up the road* from me in a marigold brick house. She had freckles and brushfire for hair, and I, enamored, turned to stare at her each day on our school bus rides. There were no pulpit sermons at New Home of damnation and condemnation about queer (or *funny* people, as we called them). That work was community outsourced. All young girls had crushes on older girls. All young girls kiss other girls in convenient experimentation. At some point, those girl crushes and girl kisses are replaced by boys. That never happened for me. Boys were rote, expected, necessary. But girls? Girls were *dreams*. Yet exile and persecution were the fates of a *girl like me*. I would have to *become* a girl who liked boys to spare myself. The summer after my fifteenth birthday, I decided to reconfigure myself into straightness. I went into our guest bedroom, lay on the floor between the bed and the papered wall of mauve birds, and replaced the girls of my fantasies with boys. I exiled myself without explicit demand or instruction. An exile of refusal.

I refused to be Pearl.

I refused to be Angie.

I refused to be Ara Jean.

I refused to be bulldagger, bull dyke, nasty, or funny. I refused it all.

There is a term that's reached the zeitgeist of the *churched*: church hurt. If there is a measure, an index of that hurt, it would be the sex I never had. The girls I never gave myself permission to love. The years lost separated me from the biology of my own body. My lungs were outside of me. I watched them breathe without me. My heart was outside of me. I watched it beat without me. My sex was outside of me. I lay down. *I lied.*

I was an imposter. A scammer of my own mind.
A poem-less Audre Lorde.
A Rosetta Tharpe without her Little Sister.

Oh, but something happened during that self-imposed exile. Something shifted, something got a hold of me: the Holy Ghost. There was only silence at first. Then it knocked because next door to that lonely room, I had a grandmother on her knees praying for me. *Wave your hands if you had a praying grandmother!*

Soon, I was a walking Pentecost in my Gunne Sax dress, white patent leather shoes, and white lace socks. I was a disturbed apiary, a tornado trail of high winds and astonished trees. In the presence of the Holy Ghost, gender falters and vanishes. It softens and creams a space. The Holy Ghost makes women of men as they cry and dance. We see it in the second lines in New Orleans, where the Holy Ghost is set free on the streets, men praising with their hips, thighs, and behinds. The presence of the Holy Ghost made men of women. They carried. They led. They held the weight of us all. Gender is mocked in the wake of the Holy Ghost. In this holy space, my sexuality was possible. Me and Carolyn Varnado were possible. *I* was possible as my future radical, queer self.

As I write this, there are billboards placed in parts of the country with my image and words: "My name is aunjanue ellis, and I had an abortion." I did this in response to the campaign of religious intimidation waged against Black women on highways all over this country. I am a Black woman who wars with raging blood against patriarchy and white supremacy. I do this fueled by the Holy Ghost and the legacy of The Mothers of New Home Baptist, the Southern Black Church Women. I must say here that I do this work outside the Black feminist space. I do not believe that "we should all be feminists," as Chimamanda Ngozi Adichie urges. Feminism has failed the Southern Black Church Woman. In the feminist space, the Southern Black Church Woman is spoken about, but rarely is she spoken to. She is seen as a dupe of T. D. Jakes and Tyler Perry, relegated to the *niche* of religious womanism. However, she is the beginning of us all, her fire forged in ship holds, hush harbors, and the Azusa Street revival. There is not one movement—civil, freedom, or Black revolutionary—that was neither led by nor made possible by *her*. The Southern Black Church Woman is not one of the overlapping identities of intersectional feminism; she is the very foundation of liberation and Black identity.

The bloodroot.

The blood.

There is power in it.

Southern Black Church Women battled men who didn't allow them to do the work of liberation in their own churches. Even now, women evangelists in my hometown are barred from pulpits, instead rising from the pews to deliver their sermons. In our church, we would have two devotions at the start of services—one led by The Mothers, the other led by the Deacons. The prayers of The Mothers were deemed insufficient. The Deacons would have to pray after them so God would show up. Yet these men were nowhere to be found in Wednesday night prayer meetings when those knees got scarred from the broken floor. This is when intercession happened. This is when the Black Church, Black people, were nursed, doctored, and fortified to survive.

These Southern Black Church Women stood up to and confronted the Black Messiahs like Rev. Dr. Martin Luther King Jr. and James Bevel, who tried to silence and render them invisible. They were sterilized against their will and advocated for birth control. They suffered the slights, the slings, and arrows that come with being Black, woman, and prophetic. They demanded more than voting rights and equal rights. As Mrs. Fannie Lou Hamer famously said, "Why would I want to be equal to someone who steals my name?" Southern Black Church Women broke ground, planted seeds, and kept communities alive from their gardens and fields. They did all this while being shot at and chased from their homes.

Think of the Southern Black Church Woman as dark matter. Scientists say the matter we know—the stars, galaxies—only make up five percent of the content of the universe. Dark matter composes the rest. We do not see it, but the power of it holds galaxies together. The Southern Black Church Woman may not be the figurehead of the Black Church, but best believe it is her work, her money, her say, her energy that holds it together, keeps it a beating heart. I am what I am—we are what we are—because of their great kiln. And *yet*.

There were two gods in that church, and they were at war. One told me I was a "wretch undone" and I needed to be "washed as white as snow." The other didn't speak with words. This god held no written scripture and verse but prayed loving arms around me. A god that held me with loving hands that flung me into the clouds, having already fitted me with Black wings to fly. Two gods: biblical god v. *BlackGod*.

The white men and women who waged a campaign of lynching in Mississippi were praying folks. Church-going men and women who diligently prayed before they murdered Black mothers, fathers, and children. Their victims prayed too. They prayed to be spared. Prayed for the families they would leave behind. Prayed that after their horrible deaths, Heaven would be their home. Is this the same god? No. *No, no, no, no,* **no**. John the Apostle declares that, "In the beginning was the word . . . and the word was God" (John 1:1 KJV). If this is how the word becomes flesh, the word cannot be the Bible. What a woeful, unfinished document. How impoverished the Bible is in its capacity to meet the times. The Bible is little more than an abject celebration of genocide, infanticide, and bigotry. Its only utility is as a ledger of God's violence. Where are the numbers? Where is the accounting of Black bodies murdered by the Bible's Curse of Ham? It is a number we will never know.

We talk of Black Jesus. We laugh at the absurdity of a white Jesus hiding in the depths of North and Central Africa. But what about the Father/Mother? What we say less is what I'm most certain of: God *Herself* is Black. Artificial intelligence and Google have made the omniscience of the biblical god redundant. Being all-powerful, all-knowing is insufficient for a *BlackGod*. It ain't enough. Even seven-day creation is not enough.

BlackGod asks, "Where is your art? Where is your Faith? With her rings of gold. Where is your mutinous Titus Kaphar?" *BlackGod* overthrows King James and puts Prince on the throne. *BlackGod* asks, "Where is your laughter that makes you run when no one's chasing?" It asks, "Where is your community that feeds from its gardens?" It questions the place of justice for SandraTamirBreonnaGeorge . . . and demands we sit in *selah* of what horrors lie in this three-dotted ellipsis. *BlackGod* demands a fight not for mere freedom but liberation. Freedom is the white man's folly. Freedom has no morality. *BlackGod* demands a "getting free" that is inextricably tied to community. *BlackGod* restores a Black woman's body from a political site and the endless siphoning for cultural production and labor. *BlackGod* sees her as whole, precious, needed, and gives her rest.

Black folks made God good. We gave God song and morality. We made God beautiful. The Bible *is not* my evidence of God; the speculative fiction survival of Black folks *is*. The cosmos we built over and under the Atlantic is. *This* will always have me trying to find a church on Sunday morning. I yearn for the word of that survival's testimony. So I turned to the queer woman preacher in

Atlanta who said, "God has given us all the hands in Ella and Fannie and Nina; there are no more hands to give." I turn to the wordless improvisational prophecy of Dorinda Clark-Cole and to her sister Elbernita Clark-Terrell for the witness of Black Woman Existentialism in "Is My Living in Vain." I turn to the ministry of Toni Morrison, Imani Wilson, Christina Sharpe, Camonghne Felix, and the queer poet t'ai freedom ford. I turn to the visual work of the Black ecologist/artist Allison Janae Hamilton. I read from *the Word* of Lakiesha Carr. "Fill the eyes with hot water. Lava," she writes. "Become a volcano. Become the ocean, the unexplored depths. Be woman. Be Black."

Seeking the Word was what brought me to Pastor Danyelle Thomas. Lockdown. It was only months after I had lost my best friend, my reason for life, my mother, Jacqueline Taylor. I needed *claiming*. I found it in Danyelle. I was looking for another Southern Black Church Woman, someone bearing the same scars and joy. I found it in Danyelle. During this time, I was in a movie about the seismic music of the migrational Southern Black Church Woman, *The Clark Sisters: The First Ladies of Gospel*. I was looking for wisdom as I tried to discuss these national treasures. I found it in Danyelle. Of Elbernita Clark-Terrell she wrote, "We owe it to Twinkie, to ourselves, and our daughters a faith wherein freedom to be whole and holy is not relegated solely to an eternal gain. This conversation of a reconciliation and liberation of both the faith and its adherents matters, has mattered, and will always matter." I saw in Danyelle a preacher who saw the dismembering practice of the biblical god, particularly when it came to Black women. A preacher who sought to reunite us with what had been separated from our souls, our resplendent but maligned bodies. A preacher who did not see body and soul as antonymic, as opposing forces where one must choose to serve a true and living God. A preacher whose brilliant mind always invited me in without condescension or pandering. I am so honored to know her, to call her, as Morrison describes in *Song of Solomon*, "a friend of my mind."

At New Home, we would prepare for the Word by standing and singing "Amazing Grace." It is time again for a song of preparation, but we need a new one for Pastor Danyelle. No, we need a few. We will start with Jazmine Sullivan's 2020 BET Awards performance of "Pick Up Your Feelings." We will sing it not as a song about a mere f-boy we are discarding but as a song of refusal of all and anything that would abase us. Sister Beyoncé Knowles will bless us with our anthem during the Supreme Court attack— "Church Girl"— rebuking unjust rulings against our bodies. She'll declare that we were born free, that our liberty was never at the mercy or judgment of white sovereignty. Finally, B'ethel Church will bless us with "I've seen HER do it, and **right now**, it's working out for me."

Let's get ready for the Word, y'all! It's getting ready to happen. THE NEXT VOICE . . . *it's getting ready to happen* . . . YOU HEAR WILL BE . . . *it's getting ready to happen* . . . Pastor Danyelle Thomas.

Her voice . . . *it's getting ready to happen* . . . it got the blood in it . . . *it's getting ready to happen* . . . there is power in it . . . *it's getting ready to happen* . . . wonder-working power!

It's getting ready to happen!

Preach, pastor!

Preeeeeaaach!

aunjanue ellis-taylor is an artist, activist, and film, stage, and television actress and producer. She is—in skin and intention—a

Blackity-Black-Black BLACK radical queer woman forged in the beauty, wonder, and wounding of Southern Black Churched Womanhood in McComb, Mississippi. She is best known for her storytelling of the legacies of Black women through her portrayals of Oracene Price in King Richard *(2021), Hippolyta Freeman in* Lovecraft Country *(2020), Dr. Mattie Moss Clark in* The Clark Sisters: First Ladies of Gospel *(2020), and Isabel Wilkerson in* Origin *(2023).*

PURGE ME,
WASH ME

Overdose

Too much of a good thing is always a bad thing
Bible school taught me that pastor and pusher could
be one in the same
I was made addict before I had permanent teeth
And eventually I overdosed on church

They rushed me in,
Pumped my stomach,
Hell, fire, and brimstone spilled out
And all this time I thought it was the Holy Ghost

Sundays felt so good
We looked so good
Venom tastes just like grape juice
Bondage can look like crushed wafers
Indulgence is so innocent until it isn't

Cash Money Deacons shouting barbiturates from
hymnals felt so right
Until I watched turf wars take casualties between pews
and knew I had to change

I never left God
I just needed to get clean
The first step of my detox
Was to stay home on Sunday
And my symptoms were under control

Until my organs crashed
Fire spilled out
I'm still staring at the color
Still looking at my organs
Frankly
Wondering if there's anything holy left

—Valerie B

1

Did Not Our Hearts Burn?

I'VE NEVER DONE HEROIN, but I've overdosed on the Holy Ghost, and that first Sunday morning I chose to forsake my lifelong ritual of attending church felt like fighting through the cruelest of withdrawals. Fearfully, I chose to lie prostrate in bed instead of on the sanctuary's altar, defying every fiber in my body, fiending for a dopamine fix that only the assembling of the saints could give. There is no greater love I have ever known than my love for the institution of the Black Church. It is a love that bore the burden of my heavy heart and gave refuge from the condemnation of my Black body in this life. It has also broken my heart and connection to self, terrified of questioning God lest I be held in contempt. It is a love that has often required me to see myself as a wretch undone and whose purification of my womanhood and sexuality nearly left me at irreconcilable odds with both. When I began my exodus from the church, I'd already been contemplating where the God of my youth fit into the evolution of my twenty-something adult life.

My once peerless religious faith met its match between textbook pages and lecture halls, deepening my understanding of the very world that I'd been taught to fear in the pews of my sanctuary. My lifetime of "because the Bible tells me so" did not stand a chance in the crude enlightenment of my psychology courses on sexuality and social behaviors. Hours of lectures, research, and writing to fulfill the requirements of my Africana Studies major pushed me to question why my Blackness, in the sight of God, was a condition whose punitive symptoms could only be remedied by adapting to whiteness. I was no longer satisfied in waiting for absolution by death in this life in hopes of reaching Heaven in the next one. By the time that fateful Sunday came, the interrogation of my faith gave way to my seemingly simple decision to abstain—at least for this one day. The choice sent a hellish, heaving guilt coursing through my body. In that moment, my contradiction of a lifetime of dutiful, unquestioned devotion left me fully assured that my mind was turned reprobate and my soul condemned to hell. The simplicity of my "no" that morning could never capture how profoundly bitter it is to completely reject all you know to be true.

I was raised in the psychological terror of apocalyptic fear in the era of the *Left Behind* series. My ethics were defined by a culture that valued spiritual readiness for the return of Christ at any given moment. Death, incapacitating illness, or acts of God were the only plausible reasons a good Christian should miss church. Yet here I was, exercising my option to skip simply because I *wanted* to do so. My anxiety was unrelenting, each thought creating a new ominous scenario of God's wrath upon my soul that sent waves of agony through my stomach. I'd never felt so alone, so isolated, as I did then. The world outside seemed to have faded away, leaving only the relentless torment of my body and mind of what it meant to have committed an unforgivable sin. The momentary satisfaction of my defiance seemed like a cruel joke now, mocking me as I lay there writhing in mental anguish. Like an addict, I sought solace in any way to ease the pain of the cravings that seemed to come in crashing waves from the depths of my soul. I could hear their siren song through my rationalizing that it was not yet too late to back out of this choice. My mind whispered hopefully, *You can still make it close to on time, maybe just a few minutes late*, seeking relief from the endless agony of withdrawal.

That moment in time not only surfaced my deepest fears but broke open a freedom I'd never known. The loss of my religious rhetoric and dogma as I knew it left me free to question in ways I never had before. Finding a new experience of God beyond the one I'd inherited was like standing on the edge of a cliff, gazing out into the abyss. I could turn back, but that would only lead me to beliefs whose comfort now seemed hollow and meaningless, their promises of salvation ringing false. To go forward in a world that suddenly seemed dark and uncertain left raw, gaping wounds that I worried I would not have enough of God left in my heart to heal.

But oh, how my soul loves Jesus. The memories of my young Sunday mornings smell like those of a favorite old lover, complete with the tingling sensations of their indelible imprint on my senses—the nostalgia of pale morning sunlight seeping through windowpanes, signaling my Sabbath's arrival. My awakenings soundtracked by *Bobby Jones Gospel.* I can even taste the memories of breakfasts with Mama's thick grits lining my belly for the marathon of hours to go before the reward of after-church dinner. It all still fills me with joy, even amid my disillusionment with the faith of my youth. The raising of hymns in Daddy's Baptist services was a tender caress like none other. The slow buildup as congregational voices rise to match the timbre of the deacons leading us through each line, keeping time with the pulse of double clapping. The foot stomping that sent the elders into a *Baptist fit* of uncontainable possession, bending their bodies, and pitching their screams to heights that can only be described as ecstasy. Indeed, God has been just that good.

My parents' divorce made me definitively *Bapticostal*, and Mama's charismatic Pentecostal roots are as much part of my foundation as those Baptist Sunday School classes on the weekends I spent with Daddy. The storefront church we called home for so long was nondenominational—on paper, at least. In practice, it was Pentecostal in every doctrinal way *except* having accountability to a governing body. The familiar organizational hierarchy of trustees, deacons, and clergy of my Baptist experience flattened in Mama's church, leaving the Bishop as the self-appointed presiding prelate, our highest and final authoritative voice of God's word. My church home became the base camp of my deepest spiritual wounds. A place where my pastors' spiritual abuse often muffled God's call on my life. Yet, recollections of goodness I found in our community of believers wash over my being like the warmth of an exquisite morning in the summer sun. Intercessory prayers in unknown tongues were followed by frenetic, enthusiastic praises to God through song. When we reached the final notes, our feet danced until we passed out drunk in the Spirit. Even when rendered asunder by the heartbreak of a perilous faith, my heart still burned within.

If I believed in the concept of soul ties, none would be stronger than the cord between mine and the Black Christian tradition. Almost nothing feels as deeply sensual as the intimacy in the spirited high of a deliverance service. I struggle deeply with the shame of that truth. It betrays every self-denial and pleasure-repressed bifurcation of the sacred and the sensual that my love affair with the church worked so hard to reinforce. From the moment I step into the sanctuary, it is an experience that beckons my total surrender.

The invocation to worship is delightfully overwhelming to all my senses. The rhythm of our opening congregational medley keeps our bodies rocking in perfect time to our syncopated clapping. The musicians play familiar chords that serve as the underpinning of every *Have you tried Jesus* and *I'm a soldier in the army of the Lord.* Their loud, bright sounds create a sense of energy and excitement within us. The repetitive melody stirs our sense of expectation, inciting our longing for the pouring out of *His* spirit. By the time the medley has tried Jesus and found Him to be *alright, alright* in its refrain, we are fully primed for a move of God. The joy of devotion ignites a slow-burning flame deep within us, a spark of energy that flows throughout the body. Our hearts are poised in anticipation, and every sense is heightened as if the world is more vibrant, more alive than it was mere minutes ago.

After we've been raised high, we are invited deeper into worship with minor chords and driving, unresolved harmonies building rhythmic momentum and musical breakdowns whose tension punctuates our defenses and evokes tears of release. Indeed, the presence of the Lord is here in our corporate worship, where I hear deeper longing tucked within heartfelt lyrics of desire not only for the infilling of Spirit but also for the romantic intimacy we often deny ourselves in the crucifixion of our flesh for *His* namesake. Instead of yielding to temptation, we often place the longing in the music where it can be cared for and sanctified in ways that the confines of chastity in pursuit of holiness would never allow.* This kind of worship experience *edges* us, bringing us almost to our peak but suspending the finish for more intense pleasure. Without resolve, the instrumentation stops and is replaced with whispers, wails, and deeply passionate expressions of praise. It is the final

---

* Personal correspondence with Dr. Ashon Crawley, 2022.

switch that unlocks the connection between the individual and the divine, one that has been forged by complete surrender.

With the atmosphere set, the anticipation of something big is *palpable*, and our spirits are poised to receive the word through the messenger of God. As the preacher feels their help coming on, the tuning up of *preaching chords* from the organ births energy that becomes a consuming fire of every thought and feeling carried with us into the sanctuary, leaving nothing in its wake but raw, primitive vulnerability that engulfs our bodies with longing for more of this pure, unadulterated bliss that fills every fiber of our being as the sermon crescendos to its closing climax. The tender aftercare of an altar call, complete with a healing touch, is the sweetest finish. No wonder I felt compelled to return one Sunday after the other just to feel this *alive* again.

There is an old spiritual that contends you can "weep like a willow, you can moan like a dove. But you can't get to Heaven lest you go by love." With deep, abiding love, I set my sights on Heaven as a glorious promise of respite from this life of class warfare, misogyny, and oppression grounded in anti-Blackness for the upkeep of the hegemonic empire. Heaven became a promise that we'd understand the trials and tribulations of this life, a reward so good that it would be worth the abject suffering and impoverishment of our earthly existence. Heaven was the reason to disempower ourselves from sociopolitical action because we don't need to be of the world while in it, but remain vigilant in knowing that this life will be over while Heaven lasts always.

Admittedly, its winding contradictions and insufferable hypocrisy make a strong case for our collective release of the Black Church tradition as the rotting fruit of colonization. I'm inviting you into my search for the light of God in darkness formed by the shadows of sexist, classist, and anti-Black imaginings of God. By the grace of reclaiming my autonomy from the grips of death-dealing theologies, I've seen the light of liberating truth. I'll tell you stories grounded in both works cited and a deep soul knowing of my truth. You'll witness my reclaiming the authority of my lived experiences as *enough* to rename who God is to and for me. I'll break it down so that it may forever remain broken: Blackness is holy in and of itself.

What is inherently Black and othered is not in desperate need of the salvation of supremacist ethics. It does not need to be washed white as snow to be witnessed as faithful. My faith comes from hearing my ancestors' testimonies of God. In being stolen from their homelands, customs, and communities, they fought to keep and carry the memories of home. They preserved those memories by placing them in what are now the distinguishing features of Black religion. I hope that at the end of these pages, you too will search for a divinity that sees you just as you are. But first, I have to tell you the story of trying to love a holy God who did not see me as *whole*.

My relationship with the institution is lovingly *complicated*. It can only be love that soothes my spirit while lining my father's beloved rendition of "A Charge to Keep." My inexplicable recall of the precise meter of these *Zion* songs, even though I don't quite remember ever being formally taught, justifies my faith in that love. When nothing else could help, the church's imperfect love lifted me. Out of love, the church mothers and ushers taught me to mind my hem lengths and to keep a proper lap cloth for the sanctuary. Even though I know that beneath this agape love was religious dogma rooted in patriarchy that held women and femmes responsible for the uncontrolled lust of men, it was out of a healthy fear of God's wrath that they fostered my ignorance through the imperative to *not* question God, being taught instead an acceptance that His ways are not our ways. They told me that Jesus was the lover of my soul but showed me that it was a precarious connection under seemingly constant threat by my soul's sin sickness, weakness, and brokenness brought upon by my struggle to stay the straight and narrow way.

My realities within it punctuate my undying love for this tradition. I was nearly convinced that if it could not consume all of me, only the fiery lake of hell could. It is a love that has covered a multitude of sins against my own best interests committed in God's name. I am painfully aware of how this indulgence of the cross has both saved and failed us. The institution built and sustained by our hands which saw us through Jim Crow and the civil rights movement often seems to have abandoned us to the devices of a colonized Christ more interested in unquestioned obedience than the liberation of the oppressed. We are encouraged to pursue Black Excellence that is little more than a white aspiration, building our hopes on the sinking sand of assimilation as salvation from the conditions of our race and, for many of us, gender and sexual expression. Devotion to white evangelical theology has rendered a church more obsessed with whom we lie down with than whom we're fighting against the structural inequities that persecute us on every side. We've yielded our power of creation to our oppressors, who called it demonic witchcraft *just* for the chance to reach a Heaven we never seem righteous enough to enter. When the push of reason comes to shove my uncritical faith into the stark light of methodical inquiry, what remains is a complex love that is complicated by the residue of its baptism in white supremacy. But who wants a perfect love story anyway?

> Purge me with hyssop, and I shall be clean;
> wash me, and I shall be whiter than snow.
>
> —Psalm 51:7 (NRSVUE)

· 2 ·

White Man's Religion

CONTENT WARNING (CW): CHILD SEXUAL TRAUMA, PARRICIDE (FAMILY VIOLENCE) & SUICIDE MENTIONS

I DO NOT AND *CANNOT* subscribe to faith in a God that ignores how race, class, gender, and other forms of oppression intersect and compound, nor one that asks me to do the same. *Christian* does not become a substitute pronoun for my Blackness, womanness, and other intersecting margins. Being Black *and* Christian means also grappling with a religious tradition plagued by racism, sexism, trans- and homoantagonism, and systemic oppression. I am not interested in defending or apologizing on behalf of Christian harm. I believe that objections to and criticisms of Christian beliefs, apparent contradictions, and inconsistencies are necessary for accountability. I do not identify as a Christian in denial of its harm because I believe dismantling the Christian evangelical legacy of anti-Blackness, misogyny, and colonialism within our spiritual practices is what I've been called to do.

> When the missionaries came to Africa they had the Bible and we had the land. They said, "Let us pray." We

closed our eyes. When we opened them we had the Bible and they had the land.

—Bishop Desmond Mpilo Tutu

There are two things I believe to be true: there are no white people in the Bible, *and* as is customary of whiteness, the biblical narrative has been revised and wielded as an effective instrument of social control—and struggle.

Before some of you morph into conservative news commentators decrying false witness of "reverse racism" and Black supremacist rhetoric, hear me out. There are no white people in the Bible because whiteness is nothing more than a political construct absent of both ethnic and national origin. Inarguably, the Christian faith has been wielded to reinforce the power of a supremacist state. This truth is one of many contradictions I've had to reckon with within my work of religious reconciliation. Still, I'd argue that Christianity is not "the white man's religion." The state religion of whiteness is, in fact, the acquisition of power through capital—real and imagined. Christianity merely serves as a convenient institution that convinces us that it is the will of God to further its cause.

God is good all the time; and all the time, God is good.

My compulsory Christian faith in the goodness of God has been woven into the fabric of every aspect of my existence, from how I understand the sociopolitical conditions of the marginalized to the critical thoughts I've allowed myself to have about God's role within them. I never decided if *I* believed this edict; it was simply a non-negotiable truth.

Truthfully, I'm not sure that God is always *good*—or that I even need God to fit the dichotomy of good or bad. I do know with absolute certainty that it is not to my benefit to ignore the negative emotions birthed by complex lived experiences in favor of performative Christian happiness. I also know that this *cultural norm* manipulates my love for God to my detriment. God doesn't benefit from my facades of happiness in the face of economic exploitation, political disenfranchisement, and cultural erasure. Still, my willingness to accept my condition as a heavenly mandate helps to reinforce inequality.

Call and response mainstays like *God is good* stem from a tradition that speaks to the power of community and collective expression, of voices joined together in cultural agreement that regardless of what happens in our lives, God is good in and through it. That questioning otherwise is an act of betrayal against a faultless God. It is a clarion call to seek the goodness of God within the worst experiences. It is a universally resonant response in which we can hear the echoes of generations past, the voices of those who have gone before us, to keep our dignity through the worst of adversity and keep the faith amid abject failure. Yet when someone leads the call of *God is good*, I rarely think to question my responding declaration that this goodness is always without failure.

The most important indoctrination of the Christian experience is assimilation into its emotional culture. We are taught to speak of ourselves as happy, satisfied, and complete because we, unlike worldly others, have a relationship with Jesus, which makes everything alright. Our Christian faith is as much a coping mechanism for the horrors of human experience as it is intended to be a saving grace for them.

We are taught that we can only achieve happiness by abandoning ourselves in favor of new Christian behaviors, e.g., nonmarital abstinence and political apathy. This happiness, in turn, proves the authenticity of our transformation, an unassailable sign of the "power in the blood." Happiness becomes not only a reward for the faithful; it is a prerequisite for communal acceptance and an essential component of a healthy Christian witness.

To continue our appearance of being "right with God," we are taught to limit negative emotions like anger and sadness, regardless of life circumstances. Rote memorization of scripture and clichés about the character of God are primary methods of our emotional control toolkit. The difficulty of these expectations up the ante—the harder the circumstance, the more triumphant in God we are when generating relentless positive emotions. Compulsory Christian happiness is symbolic in its social controls or boundaries and serves as Christianity's most moral emotion. We're taught to define these controlled emotions as *happiness*, to see all of life with the unquestioned joy of the Lord. But even emotional cultures that are experienced as positive can create and maintain inequality by rewarding subordination, justifying domination, or masking internal hierarchies.[1]

Not all my church memories are traumatic nightmares. Some, I'm quite fond of, in fact. The afternoon when I lay face-planted in my homeboy's front yard is one of those.

Small churches really do end up becoming your extended family. These folks become your community of believers that if we stick together in this faith, we'll *all* be free someday. Even though the love created in these spaces is sometimes flawed, it is earnest in its sincerity. For one reason or another, we always found ways to fellowship beyond Sunday service. Wednesday night Bible study sometimes happened at Sister Nissey's house, where all the kids would be allowed to go upstairs during the sermon, and our parents were happy to be free from our distractions. Chris and I were *church* friends. But our mothers were close—in age and lived experience of healing single mothers—so that made us cool too.

I adored his mother as much as I feared her. Simply put, Ms. Janice didn't take shit and was not to be played with. Maybe because her no-nonsense demeanor was so similar to Mama, I saw tenderness where others saw unfiltered bluntness, but I always found her to be incredibly kind. Once you understood not to try Ms. Janice, you knew you'd get the best of her. She always told my mother she wanted another child—a daughter—despite still being single and prospectless. I knew Ms. Janice was gonna have that baby with or *without* a husband. Because she was too tough not to go for what she truly wanted. Even *life* knew not to fuck with Ms. Janice.

There's something to be said about the youthful lack of mortal awareness. That could be the only reason I let Chris talk me into *tying* a leash from a skateboard to his bike and riding down that steep hill. In my defense, not only did it sound *hella* fun, but I also figured by being the driver of the *bike* that I was mitigating my injury risk; the one with the brakes would be the safest bet. And that's how I ended up planted face down in Ms. Janice's front yard under a trampled bike. Chris let go just before things went south. We had this kind of inside story we'd spend a lifetime laughing about in those awkward moments we'd sporadically connect over social media. If he were here, we probably would be reliving that story for the rest of our lives.

I stood before five caskets in 2016, the year I've dubbed my personal *Hell Week*. In January of that year, my beloved Daddy and a childhood pastor died exactly one week apart before the age of sixty. By November, the other three coffins were laid in a semicircle at the church's altar. I hadn't planned to come, but I just so happened to *accidentally on purpose* be in the area. Agony compelled me, and grief convinced me to be there that day. And I can't fully explain why the sobs wracked my body when they carried out Ms. Janice, Chris, and the daughter Ms. J always wanted whose life was stolen too soon at the tragic end of a murder-suicide. Because even though we weren't that close, the Chris I knew my entire life would never take the lives of the mother and sister he loved. Yet, I had to accept that he was some kind of a complicated villain.

During the remarks portion of the service, Ms. J's husband spoke. She eventually married her daughter's father shortly after her birth, doing exactly what I always knew she would do her way. He spoke with deep compassion about his stepson, who stole his lover and child in one fell swoop with no satisfactory explanation. Chris's other sister followed him. Until that day, I had no idea she even existed. Chris and I were a lot alike. Chris shared a father with his sister but, for all intents and purposes, had been raised as an only child. She took the podium and, after clarifying her relationship with the deceased, said the most profound thing I've ever heard in my life of witnessing Black funeral rites. She said, "Chris, what I'm most glad to know is that the last of you is not the best of you." Considering the circumstances, the gathered mourners met her tearful remarks with surprising tenderness.

When we do not interrogate God's perpetual goodness, we become obligated to find goodness in the most inhumane of circumstances. Like in the destruction of Black Wall Streets in Tulsa, Oklahoma, and Memphis, Tennessee, and in South African apartheid. And in the violent aberration of the transatlantic slave trade where unspeakable horrors are recorded in our ancestral memories. Within the broken bonds of love between parents and children by homophobic vitriol fueled by infallible scriptures, God must be *good all the time*. In the dismal maternal outcomes of Black mothers and children, with diminishing opportunities for the sustained economic, physical, and social health and wellness of these families, *all the time* God still must be *good.* And while looking at three caskets, a sister must still find the goodness of God in the violent shooting deaths of a mother and her ten-year-old daughter at the hands of her troubled brother.

I needed to believe that God was *still good* amid my first unwanted sexual contact at seven years old when the dark-colored Jeep Grand Cherokee pulled into the parking lot of Avondale Mall where Mama left me in the car parked in front of the mall's entrance while she ran a quick errand inside.

I thought nothing of it as the vehicle pulled up. I followed Mama's instructions: keep the doors locked and stay in place until she returned. But locks don't keep out every danger, and that unsuspecting summer day brought a darkened shadow of my psyche that would never see light quite the same again. The driver, a white man who looked to be in his mid to late sixties, exited the vehicle, never breaking eye contact with me. The mall was in a working-class Black neighborhood, so his presence was well out of the ordinary. I didn't have the language then, but I'm sure this was an intentional decision to use our Black neighborhood to find his next target. He was a predator, and I was his prey. His mission in that parking lot was as intentional and disturbing as what he did next.

In broad daylight, he dropped his pants and stole my innocence. His flaccid penis became engorged in his hand as he deliberately stroked himself, seemingly more aroused as the horror etched deeply on my face. The tears stained my cheeks as I stared at him through the window, unable to process what was happening to me and, more importantly, why. When he'd satisfied himself, his sadistic laughter was the last I saw of him before watching him peel out of the parking lot.

I didn't need God to be good. Goodness is only morally relevant to the societies that define it. I needed God to witness *all* of me. I needed God to see another Black girl being initiated into her fictive kinship of Black womanhood, where sexual trauma is a rite of passage. I know the moment in the lives of every sista I've loved where they crossed the threshold from a girl into someone's bitch or hoe who was *asking for it*. I needed God to seethe in anger, seeing a child where the world saw Black skin presented in a female body and decided she was adult enough. I needed God not to be good but furious that I'd been denied childhood innocence because I'd been born in a body never quite recognized as childish. I needed God to be good and *goddamned* mad that instead of justice for my experience, I'd spend years minimizing it as not so bad because "at least he didn't rape me." I deserved more than to be handed religious delusions that demanded I find a silver lining where the embers of rage deserved to burn freely. What I needed, above all, was a God who did not see my race and gender as negligible in His sight. Especially while I lived in a world where those identities made me irreplaceable and disposable—depending on who needs to use them for their advancement. But my indoctrination did not leave room for a God like this. Those who benefit from my oppression are better served by my devotion to a God who is always good, always just, and always above reproach. *All the time.*

Your visceral response right now is my point. The sanitation of traumatic experiences as being for the glory of God is neither uncommon nor remarkable for *churched* folks like me, and I'm painfully aware of how contradictory my religious faith and lived experience appear. The culture and, frankly, God that I've described to this point don't seem worth defending, *much less* like one worthy of devotion. Like many, I was conditioned to accept a sadomasochistic relationship—deriving pleasure from the infliction of physical or psychological pain on another person, oneself, or both—with a God whose nature is most often characterized as loving, gracious, and kind. I have lived in the narrative of an all-knowing God that will destroy you physically, emotionally, socially, and financially just for the opportunity to heroically restore you in the victorious end. My religious indoctrination normalized suffering and pain not only as inevitable but also as a signifier of holiness. In the sanctification of our suffering, we stop questioning our harm and correlate it as a necessary gateway to access our glory and reward.

I'd like to join with the saints as they sing, "You can't make me doubt Him; I know too much about Him," but it is what I know that drives my doubts. There is an inextricable history of racism, classism, death, and oppression in Jesus's name that is not blood-washed from the lived experiences of systemic injustices that uphold the state power of whiteness.

How is whiteness created? Whiteness is formed by self-preserving congressional bodies to create structural inequity through laws. Whiteness requires adjudication of those laws in a justice system that arbitrarily determines who is included and excluded in the protections of whiteness. Whiteness is a state power violently protected by militarized police to maintain its sovereignty in perpetuity.[2] Most of all, whiteness is maintained through religious devotion to power. Power is the product of sociocultural ideas that determine the actor's capacities, actions, beliefs, or conduct within a society.[3] As a state power, maintenance of whiteness is not only done through violent and judicial force but also through institutional, structural, and discursive means. Evangelical Christianity is an institutional reinforcement of this power.

Its theology likens xenophobic behaviors to patriotism and gendered, sexualized violence to faithful devotion. The dogma undergirds structural power by ordering members of society in relation to one another—such as masters and enslaved, employer and employee, parent and child, cisgender and trans, straight and queer, or elected officials and their constituents—and defining that order as natural to lend legitimacy to whiteness as rightfully dominant. Tressie McMillan Cottom notes that "Blackness is necessarily static as a counterweight to whiteness"[2] with respect to Blackness as both a racial ethnicity and identity. I'd go a step further to add that Blackness as an intangible spiritual representation of evil, darkness, and sin is also a necessary counterweight to the elasticity of whiteness as purity, salvation, and hope. As with any intersecting oppression, it's nearly impossible to tell where the sin of Black skin ends and where that of a blackened heart begins, but we are convicted to pursue deliverance of it all the same.

Uncritical inheritance of the Christian faith is one that makes a case for accepting oppression in this life for the delayed gratification of reward in the next. Within colonized Christian ideology, there is no more threatening evil than to be non-white, non-heterosexual, anti-capitalist, and a disruption to unquestioned power. It is a theology that "presents us as present victims of colonialism and capitalist exploitation [that ushers] in a contradiction we cannot easily ignore."[4] Unpacking and examining our beliefs start with acknowledging that our relationship to the Bible is complex. Dr. Takatso Mofokeng, a South African professor of systematic theology, explains the relationship between Black Christianity, the Bible, and liberation. First, Black Christians must contend with the positioning of the Bible—and emphasize its incontrovertible truth—as part of the *ongoing* process of colonization, global oppression, and exploitation. There is also the "incomprehensible paradox of being colonized by a Christian people and yet being converted to their religion and accepting the bible, their ideological instrument of colonization, oppression, and exploitation." Finally, Dr. Mofokeng contends that there is a "historic commitment . . . accepted solemnly by one generation and passed to another: to terminate disinheritance and eradicate exploitation of humans by other humans."[4]

Adaptation of Christianity by Black people across the globe was both a blessing *and* a problem for our ancestors, and it *remains* a thorn in our collective flesh. This paradox cannot remain unresolved for the sake of our survival and that of generations to come. The process by which a brown, wooly-haired Jesus becomes made in the image of a very white Cesare Borgia is not unusual to people who've experienced their *agua frescas* becoming spa water or cornrows becoming *boxer braids*. We often see the intellectual property, cultural imagination, labor, and creativity of non-white people whitened for capitalist consumption. This exploitation is, quite plainly, whiteness doing its expansive work of situational dominance. Whiteness is Jesus's racial ethnicity being inconsequential until he needs to be white. When Jesus is deemed white, Black and Brown people are deprived of seeing their divinity reflected in a savior who looks like them. When Jesus is nothing more than a docile figure of social rejection and persecution, his ethnicity is of no consequence to his utility by colonialism. However, when Jesus is symbolic of innocent Black men murdered by the state for the violent protection of structural and systemic power, the salvation narrative is complicated.

> For the love of money is a root of all kinds of evil, and in their eagerness to be rich some have wandered away from the faith and pierced themselves with many pains.
>
> —1 Timothy 6:10 (NRSV)

As I contended earlier, the acquisition of power and capital, real and imagined, is the *real* "white man's religion," and Christianity is, in the eyes of hegemony, the most practical tool to proselytize the propaganda of giving our lives so that the corporate state might live more abundantly. It is not by chance that of the Abrahamic faiths, including Islam and Judaism, Christianity is the *exclusive* religious tool of whiteness. It is the only one of the three faiths here that introduces the messianic concept of Jesus. Christian faith places tremendous importance on the death of Christ and, in turn, emphasizes to its adherents the necessity of death for reward. With this, Christianity offers two important narratives that aid in colonization. First, in its glorification of death, we are often spiritually manipulated into accepting the exploitation of our physical and intellectual labor for the financial gain of something bigger than ourselves. As the musical genius Elbernita "Twinkie" Clark penned while questioning her labor in "Is My Living in Vain," the reward of a better afterlife becomes the hope and coping mechanism of the exploited but *good* Christian.

Second, the narrative requires a savior for religion to successfully further the imperialist agenda. Any good marketer knows that a great sales pitch needs both a problem statement and how *your product* is the only reliable solution. Christianity offers the salvation of Jesus upon which whiteness capitalizes for exploitation while it continues creating the precarious situations we seek salvation for *in the first place*. Truthfully, the intention of messianic reverence is about a savior who would come to lead, join, and empower people to save themselves. Instead, we're given a disempowered salvation ethic that renders us useless participants in our oppression while desperately awaiting divine rescue.

Colonized Christianity is, without a doubt, complicit in the abusive nature of capitalism and the subsequent horrors committed in its name to maintain its dominance. I am neither anti-wealth nor a proponent of the prosperity gospel, *and* it is imperative to understand why Ecclesiastes contends that "money answers all things" and Timothy warns that the love of currency is the root of all evil. Mania love is an obsessive love toward a partner. It leads to unwanted jealousy or possessiveness known as codependency. Wealth inequality and poverty are deeply intentional systems designed explicitly for the evil of maintaining oppressive power, and, as such, money (capital) is the true and living god of the state power of whiteness. White supremacy experiences a mania love of money because it symbolizes power. That type of love of power, created not by divinity but intentional inequity, is the literal root of all evils we experience. Money, like power, is a social convention that can be changed and valued as we desire so long as there is mutual agreement. The politics of whiteness often use the imaginary value of money to position itself at the top of the caste system of social actors. The emphasis on money—from how we earn it to our assessment of people's characters due to the abundance or absence of it—aids in distracting us from the reality that whiteness, as a political construct and global power, not only offers no value but also introduces every ill society experiences.

White evangelicalism—the spread of thinly veiled white nationalist ideologies as the will of God—is functioning perfectly as designed as the institutional support of the state power of whiteness. Like whiteness, evangelicalism is disparate enough not to be contained by doctrine or denomination and can be found in every corner. It devours everyone, even those assumed to be within its protections. White Christian conservatives uphold rightist agendas in hopes that their freedom and families will be protected from harm while God is pleased by the legislation of their faith. In return, whiteness offers them loosened gun laws described as *freedom* while feeding them a diet of paranoia that chains them to the fear that danger lies in waiting around every corner. When the inevitable happens, whiteness will offer nothing more than its thoughts, prayers, and prepared statements that all but admit that the blood of slain children is on its hands. Their memories will become nothing more than talking points for political punditry. Their lost lives will serve only as offerings to the sacrificial altar of capital by way of irresistible gun lobbyist dollars.

In the wake of grief, whiteness will continue to expand its power through slashed public spending, lynchpin healthcare reform, and underfunded social safety nets, despite the reality that its gatekeepers often need all three. Yet, the illusion of proximal power by belonging to *whiteness* is often enough to keep them faithful to a visibly failed state.

For Black folks (and, I imagine, other people of the global majority), convincing us to recognize our inherited spiritual practices as demonic is the greatest trick white supremacy has ever pulled on us. Yet, we continue to be willing participants in the stripping and invalidation of our spiritual tools and power. Whiteness wins when we've got more fear and trepidation about our ancestors—our direct bloodline whose lives have proof and evidence—than we have in giving unquestioned devotion to a triumvirate deity whose image is often formed in Eurocentricity. The power of whiteness has often dehumanized us and demanded we surrender to its god in hopes of incremental restoration. It is a power that is both the cause and cure for why Black life requires civil and voting rights acts and constitutional amendments to exist in the US. White state power has stripped us of the ability to heal ourselves with encumbered socioeconomics and still left us holding the bag to undo the harm caused by it. Our reward has been the inheritance of a God that is "still on the throne" and in control but who seems unconcerned about our collective deliverance. After all, was God not in control when forty-nine people were killed at Pulse, a gay nightclub in Orlando,

Florida? Did God abscond the throne as the bodies of children lay dying at Columbine, Sandy Hook, and Robb Elementary in Uvalde, Texas? Did God fail to RSVP attendance while police served as judge, jury, and executioners for Eric Garner and Breonna Taylor? Indeed, Jesus is on the throne. But let's not forget how He got there. Jesus was first on the cross—where He was sentenced to death by the state. Our survival of navigating the death-dealing of whiteness often makes us cleave to the hope of divine security in God on the throne, but it doesn't negate the material, deadly consequences of unchecked power.[5]

The foundation of my religious tradition, ethic, and moral life is grounded by one dominant influence: charismatic/Pentecostal Christian rites and rituals. I formally identify as Christian+ as an acknowledgment of my integrated faith practices, including indigenous West African practices, ancestral veneration, conjure, and divination systems. My lived experience as a Black woman influences my interpretation of Christian theology, dogma, and ethics regarding gender, race, sexuality, and hegemony. In my personal decolonization journey, my statements of faith are as follows:

- God is justice-centered and demands the liberation of the oppressed from exploitative systems and structures as part of our reasonable service in community with one another.
- I believe that Jesus, murdered by the state in witness of his mother like so many Black mothers to come after her, is the embodiment of God's liberating presence in the world and that His life and teachings call us to work for justice, love, and compassion in all areas of life.
- While I hold it as sacred, I do not believe the Bible to be inerrant or infallible, nor do I believe it is exhaustive of humanity's experiences of God.

- I'm not a biblical literalist, so I am more focused on understanding the lessons of Jesus's humanity than the miracle of His divinity.
- I affirm that we are created in the image of God and that this image is reflected in the diversity of human identities, including gender, race, sexuality, and ability.
- I reject any theology or practice that perpetuates or reinforces systems of injustice and inequality, especially those based on our innate identities. I unquestionably affirm the humanity of LGBTQIA+ persons as holy, divine, and fully included in the body of Christ.
- I do not affirm biblical texts of terror that condemn and harm Black, Indigenous, and people of the global majority, marginalized genders, or sexual expression. Instead, I commit to rereading these passages in their proper historical and cultural context.

This deeply inclusive, liberatory faith is one that I've found in the remains of who and how God was taught to me. My parents raised me in fear of the Lord—their fears carved from their lived and *inherited* experiences of God. We have been conditioned to perceive God as both unconditional love and one whose wrath is not as easily tempered as it is invoked. We've acquired a theology of God by whom our ancestors' enslavement was divine providence, and diasporic colonization is part of His mandate. This God is one we've been taught sees us born of an inherently sinful nature that we spend the rest of our natural lives in atonement for, hoping that our martyrdom for the cross is enough for a coveted spot in eternal paradise upon death. It is a moral compass that points us toward unquestioned obedience and away from the critical inquiry that would cause us to ponder God's seeming favoritism toward those who often corrupt power in Jesus's name. It is an idea of God that insists you'll understand the purpose of your oppression better in the sweet by and by, where your latter will be greater. It assumes that your suffering in this life is an immutable penance for your sin of existing in a marginalized body.

A god made in this graven image of oppressive ideology is one whose maintenance of power is made perfect in our structural, systemic weaknesses, and that's the intention of its design.

• 3 •

The Preacher's Kid

CONTENT WARNING (CW): MENTIONS OF CHILD ABUSE, SEXUAL VIOLENCE & PARENTAL LOSS

A TELEVISION SITCOM FROM THE late '60s called *Room 222* starred Lloyd Haynes and Denise Nicholas. Created by James L. Brooks, who'd later bring us *The Simpsons*, *Room 222* was a half-hour dramedy that lasted five seasons (from 1969 to 1974) about an inspirational Black teacher who taught tolerance lessons to an integrated student body. Haynes played Pete Dixon, an idealistic Black teacher of American History at the fictional Walt Whitman High School, the show's central location. Nicholas's character, Liz McIntyre, who was both his on-screen girlfriend and the school guidance counselor, joined him. This show was well before my time and is seldom in syndication now, but I vividly remember my chance encounter with this scene.

Aretha Franklin, a guest star in the episode, sang this deep, funky song that included an interpolation of "Guide Me O Thou Great Jehovah." The scene is set in a place that looks more like a club than a church, filled with people who look nothing like the saints I see on Sundays. Denise Nicholas's character, Liz, is chatting with a man while they both take in Aretha's performance.

The man asks, "Who is that?"

Liz replies, "Inez Jackson, an old friend of mine who helps me run the place."

The man replies, "Is she a minister?" To which Liz replies, "No, but she ministers."[1]

It'd take twenty years for me to understand the seed God was planting in me at that moment. Like Aretha's *Inez,* I'm not a minister, but I do *minister.* I stopped in my channel-surfing tracks that day (which, if I remember the channel guide correctly, was a stop or two away from my destination: Nickelodeon) because it *was* Aretha. She was one of my Daddy's favorite singers and, as I grew up, became a favorite icon of my own. In retrospect, I came to love Aretha for the connection it created between my father and me and because she represented the possibilities of loving God *and* self out loud.

Only Aretha can comfortably move between a world where she can ask *Who's Zoomin' Who* and one where she reminds us of the hope that *God Will Take Care of You* without contradiction in either space. Aretha's duality is the unmistakably *churched* vocals on *Bridge Over Troubled Waters* performed in the decidedly not-church space of the Fillmore West. It is also an Aretha who is so unashamed of the gospel that she unflinchingly takes us right to church while singing about *feeling like a natural woman* in the 2015 Kennedy Center Honors performance that moved a sitting US President to tears. Aretha is a global icon and a textbook preacher's kid who took the gifts and pain of this lived experience and created a legacy that could deny no part of her humanity. Her unapologetic genius forces the church to reconcile its shame of her liberal sexual expression *and* her profound commitment to her God and faith. With her album *Amazing Grace,* she brought the *world* into the church culture, which, quite literally, saved her life. With that foundation, she also took the church to the world on stages and places *made* sacred by her work.

Like Aretha *and* Inez, I've taken my access and created a platform to give the most modern reflection of a liberating gospel to people who likely may not receive it otherwise. I've had the privilege of pioneering digital faith communities and building a sanctuary that fosters space for us to be fully human at every intersection of our faith. It's my anointing, my superpower. I have led and sustained an unorthodox digital ministry that has transformed many lives simply by answering the call to do the work my soul must have, but I never set out to be a pastor—in title or deed.

Daddy answered the call as a child, preaching his first sermon at nine years old. He spent his life enmeshed in all things church—traveling with the Florida delegation for the Gospel Music Workshop of America, revival hopping, and everything in between. If he had any other vocational aspirations, I was unaware of them. He lived, breathed, and dreamed of the art of preaching and the business of ministry. I was a PK— preacher's kid—from birth. My Daddy's life as a *preacher's preacher*—one who is both a professional reference and networking point for his peers—exposed the humanity of his brothers of the cloth. The church polity of power, womanizing, and celebrated philandering from the mouths of men who weaponized the text in public for acts they committed in private soured my taste for the profession.

If you're looking for a story of ghettoized dysfunction vis-à-vis a *Maury*-style tale of absentee fatherhood, I'm sorry to disappoint you. My parents wed shortly before my birth in a casual courthouse ceremony at Dad's insistence that I was not born *out of wedlock*, a nod to both the profoundly entrenched beliefs of his Black Baptist childhood and vocational path. A marriage doomed from its start, they separated by the time I turned two and divorced by the time I was six. At just twenty-six years old and only seven days after the legal end of his first marriage, my father remarried my Bonus Mom. My relationship with my dad was *complex*.

Between his devotion to ministry on the road as a traveling preacher and his new marriage, his relationship with me was often the losing choice. There were expensive Christmas gifts, but we spent very few Christmases together. There were new school clothes each year, but Mama often sat alone in the bleachers of my honor roll ceremonies. I dutifully showed up as the preacher's daughter, but sometimes my dad was almost as much a stranger to me as he was to the guest congregation. We built a love based on his vision for my life to become everything he couldn't be and my fear of the repercussions that would come from his disappointment.

I've never felt safer than in the arms of my six-foot-four gentle giant of a dad whose boisterous voice could strike both fear and comfort within me. He was fiercely protective and proud of me, wanting the best for my life and co-parenting with my mother as healthily as possible. I've yet to experience another man whose eyes light up as my daddy's did when I entered a room, always greeting me with a bellowing shout of excitement and pulling me into an embrace. He is the blueprint for what I want and refuse to accept *from* a man. As I said, *it's complex*. My childhood felt victimized by "The Call," luring him to chase it at the expense of me having an active, present dad. However, he was not my only source of pastoral trauma.

My childhood pastor first terrorized my psyche with threats of eternal condemnation. I couldn't listen to a secular song or watch movies without fear of what entered my "eye and ear gates." My pastor's wife first shamed my fat body, admonishing me for the simple halter top I'd decided to wear as being "not flattering" for my body. When I was nearly date raped at eighteen, I'd go through a toxic cycle of blaming my fat and female body firmly grounded in what I learned from the pulpit. It was pastors throughout my adolescence who condemned my intellectual rigor and academic achievement and admonished me not to believe I could "outsmart"

God. Questioning became interchangeable with heresy, making me actively participate in my own oppression. I surrendered my spiritual care to pastors who reinforced my negative money relationship, telling me in one breath that the love (and desire) of money (wealth) is the root of all evil and chastising my disobedience if I didn't pay tithes and offerings in the next breath. It was pastors, brothers of the cloth, who promised my dad to look after his children in death, who abandoned us instead. I was an adult and used to broken promises, but my brother was only fifteen. Watching a child's hope turn to hurt and settle into bitter resentment is a special kind of cruelty. The knife twists mercilessly deeper when it happens because of the actions of the Men of God.

My birth into a legacy of deep religiosity gave me little knowledge of plausible alternatives to the fear of God. I inherited the faith of not only my dad but also of my mama's devotion. Her first memories of God are enshrined in the small family church down the street from her home that she began attending at just five years old. Her adoptive parents would dutifully drop her off each Sunday at 9:30 a.m. sharp, despite seldomly attending themselves. Within a year, she'd met God and the patriarchal sexism of the Baptist church. During her tenure, the wife of the ailing pastor took his place behind the pulpit desk, leading to the exit of two deacons who refused to "sit under a woman." Still, young and impressionable, she quickly became swept up in love with the pageantry of the church's sights, sounds, and intoxicating energy.

By the age of twelve, her infatuation had grown into a full-blown love affair. She was speaking at conventions, leading songs in the choir, and being groomed and heralded for leadership in the youth ministry. For her, those Tuesday prayer meetings, Wednesday Bible studies, Friday choir rehearsals, Saturday youth days, and Vacation Bible School became both light and respite from the abuse she prayed fervently to be delivered from. Her parents, both chain-smoking alcoholics, created a chaotic home life that continued to send Mama running into the open arms of Jesus, whom she'd found in the fiery tongue talkin' of the Church of God Prophecy by the time she was fifteen.

The fifteenth year of my mama's life brought a baptism of the Holy Ghost and unspeakable betrayal. Verbal and physical abuse escalated to incestuous sexual abuse by her adoptive father. The absence of blood did nothing to assuage her brokenness and, more importantly, her questioning of a God who'd seemingly abandoned her despite her relentless faithfulness. She pleaded with God and her mother for help, but neither came to her aid. Her mother casually silenced her cries for help with half-hearted apologies and assertions that she'd misunderstood the intent of his touch. Mama would endure nearly a year of sexual violence until a massive coronary killed her abuser shortly after he'd finished assaulting her. Her faith briefly died with him that day, but it wasn't long before she found solace and purpose in the pulpit just shy of her seventeenth birthday.

Like so many others, my mother returned to what she knew under the pressure of all she didn't know. She couldn't reconcile how an omnipotent, omnipresent God could witness her soul be shattered daily, but she also could not reconcile a life *without* God. Like any Christian worth their weight of salvation, she hastened to His throne when trouble came. Her love for God was the cause and cure for the immense pain seemingly allowed by His hand—and deep gratitude for its end by the constricted blood flow of a blackened heart.

By the time I arrived in their lives, instilling the love of God within me could not have been more important to my parents. Though fragmented, my earliest recollection of church is a Sunday morning service with Daddy at Thankful Baptist Church in Decatur, Georgia, somewhere around 1993 or '94. My little body excitedly squirmed about in the sanctuary's wooden pews as the deacon's devotion ended and the choir's voices filled the place in the unison notes of "Oh Magnify the Lord, for He is worthy to be praised." Light poured into the sanctuary through its stained-glass windows, and so did the sounds of the organ as I clapped my little hands on the two and four with the saints and lifted my voice jubilantly to *call upon the Lord* with the choir. By the time we reached the chorus where *the Lord liveth,* I bounced around with unspeakable joy to declare that the *Lord reigned, blessed be the rock*. Like Mama, I was fully enamored with the sights and sounds of worship. By the time the National Baptist Convention splintered in 1994, I was in the choir stand of the newly formed New Beginning Full Gospel Baptist Church, where Daddy served as an elder now, singing in the children's choir. I was so rooted in my religious foundation that, as a kindergartener, to describe the meaning of Christmas, I told the story of the birth of Jesus as the reason for the season—a starkly different narrative than my peers' stories of Santa, family, and gifts. I was, without question, being trained up in the way that I should go.

My adolescence was filled with more of the same hyper-religious devotion and perfection of my role in the high theater of church in my parents' respective denominations. I was still a jewel in my father's crown in his introductory remarks as a guest preacher while remaining a secondary priority to the cloth. I followed in Mama's footsteps, taking on ministry leadership roles from youth ministry to worship team membership. My religious poison of choice was purity culture, and as a reward for my devotion, I was given the external validation I craved in return. The adulation of my pastors and church communities provided me with social capital, even if it was a currency with little value beyond the sanctuary.

By the time I was seventeen, I'd started my freshman year of undergrad and began the tension between secular knowledge and sacred belief. I was a first-generation college student, and nothing could've prepared me for the theological quandary of my experience. Psychology courses in human sexuality complicated my Bible-thumping *love the sinner, hate the sin* ethos. Sociology courses forced me to confront Protestant ethics of classism disguised as prosperity theology. Core classes within my Africana Studies major deepened my understanding of myself as a Black woman—a stark opposition to the whitewashed Jesus to whom I'd made allegiance through blood ritual every communion Sunday. No amount of admonishment from elders to neither question nor out-think God could slow the synaptic connections of my mind rewiring itself to a more rational, logical embodiment of my religious experience.

Neophyte seminarians are often warned not to "lose their Jesus" when beginning their academic journey. Still, it only took two years of undergrad before I was ready to break up with white evangelicalism. Indulging the fruit of my academic experience brought me an awareness I couldn't easily undo or dismiss. Though I still attended church, my Sunday sermons—once the compass of my spiritual understanding—came under deeper scrutiny for their contradictions. The rampant theological malpractice of the church was no longer unnoticed or accepted as rightly dividing the word of God. For the first time in my life, I reached the crossroads of abandoning the faith altogether or finding a way to reconcile and reimagine who God was to and for me. As I challenged my relationship with my spiritual parent, so came the reckoning with my biological one.

It wasn't until my mid-twenties—and my father's second divorce—that my dad and I began a relationship in earnest, rooted in mutual respect and trust. He did everything right to mend fences, never taking for granted that I offered him a second chance. Dad's lifelong complications from diabetes began robbing him of his sight and briefly forced me into the role of caretaker in the wake of his collapsing life. It was a role that broke open a deep resentment I'd worked so hard to swallow. His divorce from my Bonus Mom allowed me to finally become worthy of a priority slot in his hierarchy of needs in a cruel way. I found myself thrust into the position of caring for a man I felt I hardly knew while sacrificing nearly two semesters of college in the process. My heart, hidden with a commandment to "honor thy mother and thy father," waged an unholy war with a mind filled with memory records that suggested I do unto him as he had done unto me. I don't know if it was his intuition, empathy, guilt, or some combination thereof, but one day, as I dropped off groceries at his home, Daddy offered me sincere contrition and acknowledged the deep pain I felt being the one to show up when everything else he'd chosen over me fell away. He said to me, "I know how hard this is for you, Pup," calling me by a variant of his beloved nickname given to me at the time of my birth. "I am sorry for choosing my relationship over you. I chose the road over you. I broke many promises. And now I'm asking you to be here for me in ways I wasn't always there for you." His calling out of the feelings I worked so hard to conceal gave way to the healing our parent-child relationship needed. It wasn't just an apology; it was a validation of the wounds that had, to that point, felt wrong to hold.

We spent the last several years of his life deepening our relationship through hours-long phone calls, road trips, and our love of good meals. In many ways, I began to witness my father as a fully complex and nuanced human. Long gone was the man who wielded control over my life through fear. I learned my dad was a man who experienced a life of hurt, regret, rejection, insecurity, hollow triumphs, and profound sadness behind the extroversion and joy he gave the world. He began to tell me—and anyone who would listen—that I'd become his sounding board and confidante. I'd spent our lives together hungry for the light that shone through his eyes each time I entered a room, and finally, I held as much of my dad's heart as he would allow.

The night Daddy lay dying, I made my way to the hospital without deliberate speed, having become numb to the normalcy of medical emergencies. His first major episode, a stroke when I was eight or nine, led to amputations, loss of mobility, and a quadruple bypass. Sickness caused him to miss my high school graduation and forced him to leave hospitals against doctor's orders to attend my college graduations. Knowing Daddy was sick, I'd stayed in Atlanta despite my desire to relocate to Chicago, DC, and Houston at one point, *just in case* something happened to him. He died while I was stuck helplessly in traffic on an I-75 North on-ramp less than ten miles from the hospital. In a fraction of time, death robbed me of ever hearing his voice call my name again. I'd left my home so sure that *this too shall pass*. In a cruel twist of irony, traffic finally broke open and allowed me to freely drive the rest of the way to witness what remained of his *shell*.

Arriving at the emergency corridor of Grady Memorial, Mama and I walked into the small holding room for bereaved families where my uncle, brother, and Bonus Mom were already filling the room with the unmistakable wails of grief. While hospital staff gave us their best empathetic bedside manner, manufactured bereavement is no match for the weight of fresh and living grief.

Nothing could ease the reality that we were here to witness and collect remains instead of a discharged loved one. I saw Daddy's sheet-covered body wheeled past the open doorway, eliciting a renewed collective sob among us. My mother reached out to grab my hand in comfort, and for the first time in my life, I rejected my mother's unfailing love. I snatched my hand away because, in that moment, a split second that felt like a lifetime, this was a level of pain that not even God could heal. Maybe it was her familiarity with the pain of God's betrayal or her immense compassion for me, but she did not hold my uncharacteristic actions against me. The moment passed as quickly as it came, and I collapsed into her arms.

As his children, Junior and I were invited to witness him first. Even in the chaos of the moment, I knew that I did not want this to be the last image in my mind of my father. I didn't want to remember whatever the state of his remains was. My daddy was no longer there, and there were no conversations I needed to have with the shell he left behind. I still don't know, to this day, what pushed my body into the small room they placed him in. Filing in behind my brother, I quickly turned my back to my dad while the others wept and touched him as if somehow the warmth and breath of our bodies could bring back his. The glimpse I unintentionally caught of my father's body became a suspended moment in time. Beyond the intubation tubes and electrocardiogram stickers on his scarred chest, I could swear that I saw peace on my daddy's face.

It took two weeks after his death for me to finally fall apart. After the first night, I did what Black women do best: I donned my cape of resilience, deciding that vulnerability is both unsafe and unproductive. Caring for the needs of others provided blessed relief from the demand of tending to my own needs in the aftermath. As his eldest child, I shifted into autopilot to complete his final rites and rituals. I managed to stoically deal through the calls, condolence conversations, the wake, funeral, and even sending his remains to the crematory. I quickly learned that society doesn't do well with handling death. We're solution oriented, so we struggle to sit with silence, tears, and the inability to fix *this* type of loss. We often become well-meaning people offering words of comfort in calls and bereavement. I heard everything from "he's in a better place" to "God needed him more." I can't imagine a better place where

Daddy was more needed than here in the lives of those of us who loved him. We *needed* him here to witness more milestones and moments. The idea that God would intentionally cause us such pain to fill a personal heavenly labor shortage has never been one that settled well.

When someone you love dies, you begin to mark everything in your life as before and after their passing. Their death becomes the litmus test for just how bad an experience is while simultaneously hovering as metal clouds over every moment of joy. After the funeral, the world seems to return to its normalcy, leaving you in a daze wondering how no one else seems to recognize nothing will ever be the same.

Naively, I never imagined that my world would fall apart when he passed. I rationalized that the brevity of our closeness was so starkly different from my relationship with Mama that I could remain whole in his absence. I quickly learned that devastation cannot be fully gauged until impact when a frantic call to deliver news of his death came on an otherwise ordinary Tuesday night.

I've spent years grappling with the ache of loss and grief, wondering how I can forgive God for the robbery of my dad's absence when I'd just gotten comfortable with the permanence of his presence. This type of loss plunges you into a trauma that never quite heals, at least not in the sense that it no longer triggers a visceral response. It's a reality that seems to oppose what the world expects from us. There's an unspoken cultural expectation that every form of grief, even from death, has its limits on how long it should impact your normal functioning. No one explicitly says, "Get over it," but there's still an expectation that as sufficient time passes, the grief should be reserved for holidays, birthdays, and anniversaries. As time passes, sympathy wanes, and expectations of "healing" take precedence.

The reality is that grief is always the price we pay for love. And as long as love lives, so too does grief as our constant companion.

My grief walks beside me daily until it is violently awakened by the most mundane of memories, reducing me to tears. It is a wound that time never heals and, perhaps, our perception of the appropriateness of grief needs healing more than our inalienable relationship with it ever will.

More often than I care to admit, I wonder if I'll live to see my fiftieth birthday. It is one of the many gifts of survivor's grief that I've inherited since renal failure claimed my dad's life at the age of forty-seven, just shy of living as long as his mother, my grandmother, who died at forty-nine of congestive heart failure. Though their illnesses do not plague me, I sometimes measure my life in the years I might have left should the pattern of my paternal side continue through me. A morbid biological clock. In the twenty-five years my Dad remained alive after his mother's death, he lived in a fugue state of grief that found comfort only in the anticipation of his death. He spent most of my life preparing me for the end of his own life to ease the weight of his inevitable absence in my life.

In the year following his passing, I poured my grief into building my legacy. I never set out to be a pastor when I launched Unfit Christian. I was never my father's intended heir for ministry, instead expecting my brother to become the next Reverend Thomas. I only wanted to give voice and language to what I knew was an experience of more than just myself. My willingness to find my voice made me a beacon for others who needed the courage to find theirs. About a year into the formation of my digital faith community, members began to affectionately call me "Passuh" Dany, a title that caused immediate discomfort. I didn't ask to be a preacher's kid, but I certainly never intended to become a *preacher*.

I never wanted my work to be associated with the egregious harm I saw in the word *pastor*. I envision my work as liberating, challenging our experiences of God at the intersections of our faith, gender, sexuality, and race. The title of *pastor* put me in a position of power that I only ever associated with abuse and trauma. I didn't need the clout, glory, or fame associated with pastoring. I just wanted to make room at the cross for all of us, no matter how radically different our approach to God may be. Yet, I cannot effectively lead and heal in others what I refuse to heal within myself. I have spent years unpacking my baggage that made me run from this calling—and how I am called—for so long.

I do not know with certainty if my dad would be proud of my calling or horrified that I, as a woman, am doing "men's work" of pastoral care and leadership. As much as my heart wants to believe his parental instinct would supersede his doctrinal adherence to patriarchal scriptural interpretation, my faith in that belief often wavers in the darkened corners of my mind. Mama's fears for me, as both a woman and someone reared under women who pastored, has never been about my gender as much as her witness of the emotional toll this work takes on those who do it well. Despite these fears, I understand that honoring the loving affirmation of myself by my community is both an act of intentional healing and disruption of harmful power structures within our religious experiences.

I am called Pastor Dany because the way I've committed to showing up in this work allows them to reassociate "good touch" with pastoral care. I pastor because the people have decided it is what best honors what I give to the world, not me calling myself to pseudo power in search of clout. I walk in integrity, accept accountability, and yield my ego for the sake of good counsel and sound wisdom. It's the bare minimum of what we should expect with competent spiritual care, but it is so rare that it seems exceptional.

Daddy's death gave me the courage and fortitude to show up as a whole self, say yes to my purpose, and leave a legacy in this world. I've lived with the regret of not being with him as he departed this world. I've replayed the what-ifs and possibilities of timing and decisions more times than I can count. While I cognitively understand my presence, like my absence, would not have changed the outcome, a small part of me still holds hope that maybe, just maybe, if I'd been there, it might have been different. Yet as time has passed, my wonderings have shifted from if I could've saved Daddy to considering if Daddy instead chose, as his most selfless parental act, to save me. What if Daddy, as the fearless protector he often was to me, decided to spare my heart and mind of the indelible memory of watching him take his last breath and being unable to save him? I imagine Daddy chose to save me from the complex, deep grief with which he was intimately familiar. Of all his hopes for me to be what he could not be, being healthy and whole was paramount. It's an awareness that allows me to imagine his sacrifice was one of protection made from a love that is deeply unselfish and given without expectation or exception. My daddy, profoundly self-aware of his shortcomings in my life, thought nothing of choosing to commit the greatest act of love that he knew I could never return, bringing balance to a give-and-take relationship that often left me giving more than I received. Daddy chose me in the best way he could before closing his eyes. Knowing that kind of love exists for me and that it cannot be robbed by death is the greatest joy that grief has ever given me.

In many ways, if I consider these outcomes good, I can comfort myself with the thought that maybe Danny lived out his purpose here as Daddy to and for me despite the shortcomings of his humanity. Through his transition, I birthed a ministry that put me in community with lives I've changed and those that have changed my life. I imagine that, too, must be marveled as the beauty of ashes that is our constant companion of grief.

THE CHILDREN OF HAM

Color Issues

As dark as the midnight sky,
But you ain't have no problem puttin' your stars in me

As black as tar can get,
But tar is the strongest thing you trust to hold it all together

Big ole eyes
Big ole lips
Big ole thighs
Big ole hips
Big ole ears
Big ole hands
Big ole hair
Kinky instead

Although I've never seen eyes with oceans any deeper
Lips that are relied on to speak life abundantly
Thighs and hips that have carried the load, the burden, the children
Riddled with tiger stripes and lightnin' rods to show you the way
Ears that have always been responsible for hearing and interpreting the silence
Hands that hold scar and secret and treasure and create art and gold
Hair that is a protest in itself. A defier of gravity. A refusal to tame without a good fight, much like its owner

How did we ever see something so reflective of the
heart of God,
And do anything less than bow in reverence,
And give God praise?

—Valerie B

• 4 •

Do Black Lives Matter to God?

FROM THE CRADLES OF foster care to the graveyard of life sentences in the prison industrial complex, Black bodies seem to never be free of being *state property*. The birth-to-hashtag pipeline often begins with nuisance calls from Karens to police for existing-while-Black and all too often ends in avoidable tragedy. These indignities know no bounds of age. We utter the names of Tamir Rice, Michael Brown, and Aiyana Stanley-Jones in remembrance of lives that ended too soon. We witness the murder of ninety-two-year-old Ms. Kathryn Johnston in a botched police raid and the assault of Mrs. Rose Campbell, a sixty-five-year-old Black elder, dragged from her vehicle during a routine traffic stop—both victims of metropolitan Atlanta police forces. In a system that profits from our collective pain, there's no shortage of misery in the headlines that continues to raise our ire. True to cultural form, we've found humor in our distress as a means of survival. Living daily under the threat of whiteness weaponizing itself against us, we have no choice but to find joy where we can. Yet when the memes grow old and laughter dissolves into painful silence, we're still left with the same bleak reality: our humanity is precarious and subject to the audacity of whiteness within this society.

As exhausted as I am of begging white people to relinquish the power structures they've created and maintained for generations, so too am I exhausted of crying in the hope that God is indeed on the side of the oppressed. I am tired of burying my deepest fears and disappointment in our repeated regressions of progress in the hope that God is embodied in our fight for liberation. How many generations of Black people will be forced to hope for better on the other side as our bodies remain oppressed in this life?

We've worked to convince others of God's affection for us, yet we still have no deliverance to show. Our existence in this country has been both enslaved and embattled. Protection of our humanity has always been a political demagogue, supreme court ruling, and congressional vote away from vanishing. We have fought valiantly to build our communities despite the omnipresence of supremacy. We've had our thriving communities bombed, burned, and buried in the annals of history. We are then gaslit by our captors with stories of our inferiority, lasciviousness, and commodification for the sustenance of capitalism. Is our resounding answer to this a faith that we reimagine as God being the God of and for the oppressed?

It's time to ask if our Black lives matter to God. For so long, we've imagined our ultimate overcoming through the God who raised Jesus from the dead for our redemption. Is our Black skin the crimson stain that marks sin that not even Jesus's death can overcome in God's eyes? Are we God's modern Israelites in the exodus simply awaiting redemption? Or are we God's Canaanites whose land is stolen while they're slaughtered and enslaved?

I draw my reimagining of God on the rock of Black Liberation Theology. The survival of my Christian faith is contingent upon the hope that God is indeed on the side of oppressed Blacks in our fight for liberation. Yet, even Rev. Dr. James Cone, the forefather of Black Liberation Theology, acknowledges the conundrum in answering a basic question: "If God is liberating Blacks from oppression, why then are they still oppressed?"[1] Even in Cone's rearticulation of the gospel by the Black lived experience, Cone asks us not to forfeit consideration of the role that historical and social context plays in framing our questioning of and to God. And even forty years after the release of *God of the Oppressed*, current social contexts remind me that I'm still Black, still mad, and still not fully liberated.

Theodicy attempts to justify or defend belief in God as rational while enduring the evils of oppression.[2] The problem of evil involves these assumptions:

1. God is all good and all powerful (and, therefore, all-knowing).
2. The universe/creation was made by God and/or exists in a contingent relationship with God.
3. Evil exists in the world. Why?

Pay close attention here. Our first assumption is that an all-good God will automatically want to eliminate evil. Where does that assumption come from? For this, we must unpack both the *evidential* and *existential* problems of evil.

The evidential problem admits that God and the existence of evil coexist without conflict but wonders if the depth of this same evil makes a reasonable case against the existence of God as all-good, all-powerful, or all-knowing. Given the reality of global unjustified evil, there must be no God. Our assumption of God doesn't allow for the existence of evil that appears to have no redemptive purpose.

Practical, existential theodicy is more concerned with providing answers for those who suffer in specific circumstances. Often, the existential problem turns from asking why God allows depravity to what humans made in the image of God can do to alleviate suffering and evil. Likewise, the focus is on how believers should respond to God while suffering.

For how many generations have we fallen on our faces and beseeched deliverance from the heel of white supremacy? We have equated our ability to survive as salvation, yet we've preached Jesus as the messiah who, through our acceptance of Him as the son of God, will lead us out of bondage. How do we navigate that we have taught acceptance of Jesus as the path to freedom and prosperity when the only ones who have gained that are the same people who have been—and remain—those who uphold systemic oppression and marginalization? For Black folks who are descendants of enslaved people, the existential problem of evil asks where God was in the horrors of our enslavement AND what has God done to redeem us in the generations since. Where is the reason, purpose, and, most importantly, reward for our continued suffering?

How we answer the question of the relevance of Blackness to the heart of God solely depends on our relationship with the God of our understanding. Our understanding of God's characteristics is rooted in sociocultural norms. We understand who God is to and for us based on our social definitions of moral good and evil. Within American normative standards, God is characterized as both superhero and a benevolent wish granter. A superhero commits heroic acts via supernatural ability. To be a hero and not a villain, one must use that power to accomplish *good* deeds. When we idealize God in this way, we hold Them in contempt when the evil of suffering affects us individually and communally.

If we look to the biblical text for further context, we often find conflicting use of God's "superpowers" in the intervention of human affairs. There's God, the deliverer of the children of Israel, and God, the executioner of the firstborn of Egypt. By logical reasoning, this suggests that God is not all good OR that being all good doesn't automatically create the desire to eliminate all evil. I'm suggesting to you, beloved, that answering the "Where is God?" question is better asked as "*Whose* God am I experiencing and expecting deliverance from evil?"

Our experiences and understanding of God are deeply rooted in white supremacist propaganda, made more appetizing by inalienable Africanisms within our religious traditions. The experience of God for our ancestors is rooted in their cultural normalcy as villainous sub-humans who are unworthy of rescue by the superhero God of white supremacist creation. The premise of the superhero is that only good people are worthy of good deeds—and good is subjectively defined by those in power. By this logical course, how can a definition of God designed for oppression be reformed for liberation?

How do we define proof of matter to God? Is it by political advancement and power? Is it through acquiring unimaginable material wealth and "catching up" from centuries of colonization and enslavement? What will inform us of God's permanent concern with *Black lives*?

We've built devoted followings to charismatic ministries that emphasize prosperity—health, wealth, and happiness. While our pastors began to prosper beyond the socioeconomic statuses of their congregants, we *built hope on nothing less* than the promises of our prosperity despite our consistent failure to rise from poverty. In our desperation for relief, we rush to adhere to a religious ideology that centers cash, not Christ, as the promised reward for our devoted obedience. We are preached into the hope that if we are faithful, God will provide the acquisition of money and material possessions. With it will come respect, equality, and recognition of our humanity by white consciousness at large.

Religion and capitalism aren't strange bedfellows. To criticize Prosperity Gospel as a new phenomenon pulled from thin air would be to ignore history. In Max Weber's *The Protestant Ethic and the Spirit of Capitalism* (1905), Weber argues that we can attribute modern capitalism to the ethics of ascetic Protestantism. In 2012, 53 percent of Americans identified as Protestant,[3] which includes Pentecostal, Baptist, Methodist, and Calvinist churches, among others. Weber argues that capitalism sees profit as an end in and of itself; therefore, pursuing profit is seen as virtuous. Because of the shared Protestant belief in predestination—that God has already determined our outcomes before we reach them—Weber argues that early Protestants developed a need to look for clues of their salvation. Enter "success within capitalism" stage left. Weber concludes that the Protestant ethic views success, through hard work and thriftiness, as a personal duty and such success as a sign of salvation.

Simply put, the more successful one is, the more evidence of their salvation and favor by God. As we'd say in the Black Church, "Favor ain't fair." If the statistical averages of our collective indicators are of any note, maybe we're not God's favorites after all.

Daisy L. Machado states, "In reality, capitalism in the United States is a deeply entrenched ideology (belief system) that has survived and benefited from slavery, immigrant labor, and other forms of exploitation."[4] It stands to reason, then, that the trappings of capitalism—the acquisition of wealth, that is—can only survive by maintaining oppression and exploiting beliefs. The growing income and wealth divide between people of the global majority and whites make it clear that our speaking in tongues and shouts of "money cometh to me" aren't working.

Despite inadequate pay, executions at the hands of the police state, dismal maternal mortality rates, lack of housing, and lack of access to basic needs, we continue to push prosperity as God's plan. Without any irony, we push ourselves into a "belief that what we speak is equivalent to what God will do, [changing] the way we understand our present economic reality into one that is about a hopeful anticipation of the 'blessing' that is to come."[4]

Deciding where God stands on the matter of Black lives requires acknowledging how you choose to define the character of God. My understanding makes room for disappointment in God. It is a perspective problematized by positioning God as imperfect. It questions the necessity of having faith in the *perfecting* of ourselves by an imperfect God. It also forces us to interrogate why we are driven to seek salvation within the state of perfection. Why do we need perfection to acknowledge divinity, especially when what we usually accept as perfection still has imperfections?

The God of my understanding leaves room for balance. When we accept that nothing can be completely good or wholly evil, we eliminate the pressure of having all the answers. None of our environments, cultures, ecosystems, or ideas of God will ever be without flaw—primarily because we're not monolithic. I also understand the character of God as one of liberation. Whether They bring harm or not, the ability to make decisions is still effectively the human right to free will. Accepting that free will, however, also comes with being fully accountable. And, most times, we don't want to be fully accountable for our free will. Free will often means acknowledging the capability of better decisions while choosing active harm for others. This avoidance is evident in our portrayal of inequality as a mandate of Heaven and erasure of the evidence of those choices in banning books and rewritten histories.

With the lack of divine intervention in these decisions, it seems that God is content with our marginalization. We have chased dangling carrots of salvation that we signify through our homes, cars, jobs, and physical well-being. We've married religious faith to our hope of belonging within capitalism. We believe that if we work hard enough, American capitalism will provide equal opportunity for us. We undergird that individualistic hope with the belief that prosperity is God's inalienable predestination for our lives. As the oppressed, we only understand freedom through the lens of accumulated capital that buys us access to new social classes. Even when this shows itself to be untrue, instead of questioning our beliefs, we simply shift to belief in streets paved with gold and wealth untold in the afterlife. Certainly, we can't be leading these decades-long lives to wait on our just reward at the time of death.

We've sacrificed self-reliance and self-determination on the altar and replaced it with a faith that calls for loving forgiveness and reconciliation. Perhaps this is why we continue to measure the success of our contributions to humanity by the litmus of a culture that was never created to include the recognition of our right to fully exist as a people. Where is the God of the oppressed to break the yoke within us that binds us to the conditioned acceptance of white supremacy as our benchmark? I acquired the degrees and the $70,000 in student loan debt to show for them. Yet, I still feel my heartbeat quicken at the glimmer of blue flashing lights in my rear-view mirror. I still code-switch my tongue in hopes that it will allay the fears of white people who are afraid of my big Black body. I still am just a job loss away from losing middle-class status. Those accomplishments didn't give me access to the grace and ease of navigating systems created to enable life and liberty for white bodies. Nor does it reflect the glory of a God who rejoices in my liberation from institutions of harm.

If God is indeed on the side of the oppressed, why is it that the very foundation of Christianity is wrought with oppression of the adherents of the early church? Oppression is not just the perversion of the gospel at the hands of white supremacy, but it is literally the bedrock of the Christian faith. Jesus, the very son of God, was born into oppression. The Jewish community lived under occupation by an unjust regime, the same community as Jesus's parents. This same Jesus was born into poverty; His literal birth took place without the aid of community birth doulas or midwives. Jesus experienced life as an undocumented immigrant seeking asylum and refuge in a strange land. Jesus's life ended at the hands of the state who sought to suppress liberation of marginalized people His teachings might empower. Paul, though problematic he may be, spent most of his writings teaching the early church how to navigate the very real suppression of its beliefs.

Is this God of the oppressed the same Christian imagining of God who would root its global headquarters in the site of its messiah's oppressor? Was Jesus not crucified by the same Romans who had the legal authority to and preference for crucifixion? It is comforting to assume that God's favor falls first on the marginalized. We've leaned on the promise that Jesus was sent to "*bring good news to the oppressed, to bind up the brokenhearted, to proclaim liberty to the captives, and release the prisoners*" (Isaiah 61:1 [NRSV]). Yet our lives and socioeconomic status within this country reflect us as the red-headed stepchild rather than the favored.

While it is an empathetic sign that God would embody Herself in human form among the least of us, I cannot help but wonder why generations of Black people have only experienced varying degrees of sufficiency but never quite an abundance in prosperity. Jesus's birth, life, and death exemplify God's empathy on the side of the oppressed, but certainly, there is only one example needed. If we've established that God is both empathetic and sympathetic to our plight, why does it feel that we're fighting battles that were supposed to already be won by generations before us? Is it possible that this idea of God on the side of the oppressed is one of historical imagination?

What is liberation for Black people in the realization that American capitalism will never enlarge itself to include our success? Perhaps it is not that our lives do not matter to God but that She is wholly disinterested in helping us to merely endarken the face of an establishment that neither serves nor aids in the betterment of Her people. That is not to say God is anti-wealth. It is to say that She has better things to do with Her time than enable us to fight for liberation that seeks to gain access to and acquire the material trappings we've assigned as "whites only." How do we fight for our liberation in the wake that God is either disinterested in advancing capitalism at best or disinterested in us at worst?

Maybe it's time for us to admit that white supremacy will never pay us what they owe us. They never intended to. They didn't even believe they owed us respect as human beings when they began and continued the transatlantic slave trade. The literal and figurative blood of our bodies runs deep into the roots of this nation. It is time to shake ourselves from the slumber that tearful prayers lacking actionable faith, tongues that skillfully echo standard English, and earning debt-laden college degrees and an employer-matched 401K are edging us closer to our forty acres of restitution and a mule named justice.

• 5 •

Black & Ugly as Ever

INTERNALIZED ANTI-BLACKNESS IS A helluva drug, especially when the Bible is your most faithful dealer.

Anti-Blackness is the actions, verbiage, and/or behaviors that marginalize Black people. The spectrum of anti-Blackness is expansive, from the nuisance of workplace microaggressions to ten Black folks being murdered at a Tops Friendly Markets supermarket on the East Side of Buffalo, New York. Anti-Blackness is white people angry that The Little Mermaid, a fictional cartoon character, is cast by Black singer and actress Halle Bailey. Anti-Blackness is being aware of the differential success, advancement, and experience of Black people, not caring about it, and simultaneously taunting Black folks for their continued deficits because of it.

Anti-Blackness is no respecter of person, gender, or age. We spend lifetimes with the accumulated, negative impacts of these acts, where the constant robbery of our personhood is as American as apple pie. When we look to our faith for refuge and deliverance, we are too often met with affirmation that our suffering is par for the course of the *cursed* descendants of Canaan.

> The sons of Noah who went out of the ark were Shem, Ham, and Japheth. Ham was the father of Canaan. These three were the sons of Noah; and from these the whole earth was peopled. Noah, a man of the soil, was the first to plant a vineyard. He drank some of the wine and became drunk, and he lay uncovered in his tent. And Ham, the father of Canaan, saw the nakedness of his father, and told his two brothers outside.
>
> Then Shem and Japheth took a garment, laid it on both their shoulders, and walked backward and covered the nakedness of their father; their faces were turned away, and they did not see their father's nakedness. When Noah awoke from his wine and knew what his youngest son had done to him, he said, "*Cursed be Canaan; lowest of slaves shall he be to his brothers.*" He also said, "*Blessed by the Lord my God be Shem; and let Canaan be his slave. May God make space for Japheth, and let him live in the tents of Shem; and let Canaan be his slave.*"
>
> —Genesis 9:18-27 (NRSV)

This story of the curse of Canaan in Genesis 9 is a text used to justify everything from anti-Blackness and the transatlantic slave trade to, most recently, blaming Jewish people for foisting racist theories of Ham's Blackness on a willing Euro-American public.[1] This text leaves much room for people to shift its interpretation in favor of hierarchical groups of winners and losers in the game of race, sex, and inheritance. Here, the context we do not know is as important as what we do. Chapter 9 opens with God *blessing* Noah and his sons, who, in a post-flood world, become ground zero for repopulating the Earth. Later, we find ourselves in a story where a drunk-ass Noah wakes up cursin' folks, which anyone with alcoholic loved ones knows is a norm of alcoholism. We don't even know what Ham did that was so egregious that his grandaddy cursed his *child*.

Ham didn't get Noah drunk and naked—a consequence of Noah's choices. What I see when reading this text is the exhaustion of caring for a raging alcoholic who refuses to see both his addiction and the impact it has on his life. Being a persistent drunk is why Noah is bussin' it wide open in his tent without thought of passersby. Like any good drunk, he blames someone else for the embarrassment his decision has caused. Some biblical commentators assume that Ham's infraction is of a sexual nature—that by simply *seeing* his Daddy naked he has committed some kind of illicit, incestuous violation. Others suggest it may be a sexual violation of Noah or Noah's wife, Ham's parents. I'm inclined to believe that, as other scholars have suggested, "in an ancient Israelite context, the very act of gazing on Noah's nakedness could have been bad enough to merit an eternally binding curse since, according to the logic of ancient shaming, gazing subverted Noah's patriarchal authority, violated his honor, and humiliated everyone involved."[1] Within this patriarchal society, even witnessing another man's nakedness *feminizes* him. Like I said, Noah was in his drunk-ass bag of big embarrassed feelings. Nevertheless, the narrative, as written, sets up a message that the curse is *wholly* deserved, and the terrible futures that ensue are well earned—and that presents a *real* problem.

The characteristics of Canaan's enslavement set the tone for every slave system that followed it: denial of access to both ancestors and descendants and loss of sexual autonomy in perpetual enslavement. This story suggests that Canaan and his descendants were destined to lose their inheritance and their children to their master Shem and his descendants, a policy reaffirmed in later biblical law that allowed non-Hebrew slaves to be held in perpetuity. Exodus law emphasizes this: A Hebrew slave may choose to remain in his master's household if he would prefer to retain access to his non-Hebrew slave "wife" and their offspring. Such a slave was to be taken to a doorpost to have his ear pierced with an awl, a mark that changed his status from debt slave to perpetual slave (Exodus 21:5–6).[2] In other words, in a scheme set up by Todd to come to us with the bullshit, *biblical law* said that any children created while enslaved did not belong to their fathers but their masters. Imagine cursing an entire bloodline with the death penalty of perpetual enslavement—and stripping them of the ability to create their genealogical line—because someone might've glanced at yo' drunk, naked ass. *Ugh*.

So what does this have to do with Black folks? In this case, whiteness fills the gaps of the Genesis 9 narrative with facts suitable for logical leaps in favor of its continued power structures. The Bible doesn't conceptualize race in the biological, social constructs we engage in today. The Hebrew translation of the names of Noah's sons—Ham, Shem, and Japheth—are loosely associated with colors. Ham means "dark or black," Shem means "dusky or olive-colored," and Japheth means "bright or fair." Going with the theory that these three repopulate the earth post-flood, it is thought that each is the ancestral father of present human ethnicities associated with the skin colors connected to their names.

With a little razzle-dazzle of historical geography and biblical literalism, since both the Egyptians and Ethiopians are in the biblical record as descended from Ham, literalists identify him as the ancestor of all Black people. This designation allows the *Curse of Canaan* in Genesis 9 to be a theory of "natural" servitude for lil' Black Canaan with *very obvious* racial overtones. It is the first but certainly not the last time Canaan will be villainized in the text.

Biblical writers will almost entirely stigmatize Canaanites as sexual deviants from their introduction in Genesis to the Holiness Codes of Leviticus, where Israel is warned to avoid behaving "as they do in the land of Canaan" or risk being "vomited out" (Lev. 18:3, 25). Conveniently, both descendants of Ham—Egyptians and Canaanites—are deemed as reprehensible sexual deviants. To make the connection here, sexual deviance has *also* been used to justify present-day anti-Blackness. For Black men, assumed hypersexuality fuels both the Mandingo cuckolding fantasies of non-Black others *and* the fears of the *big, bad Black rapist* that fragile white womanhood must be protected from. For Black women, it is the persistence of the *Jezebel* sexual stereotype that remains inescapable despite personal sexual decisions.

Many slaveholders not only identified as Christian and subjected their *properties* to conversion, but also saw no conflict between their *violence* and their Christian faith. More than that, through the interpretation of its ideological instrument, the Christian Bible gave permission to both subdue and "buck break" these Black bodies into docile workhorses through cruel, inhumane violence when "biblical order" was not followed. Within *their* Christian faith, white people never intended our Black asses to rise above perpetual enslavement, and these same ancestors you've been convinced to name as demonic *knew* it in their lifetime too.

Despite having arrived on these *Christian* shores two centuries prior, most enslaved Black folks had not converted to the faith as late as the 1800s. Many of our ancestors understood that being cut off from their legacy was, in no uncertain terms, an eternal death. They fought to continue to adhere, as much as possible, to their African ancestors' religious beliefs and rituals, including the syncretic practices that remain between us and our love for Black Jesus today.

While we scream about victory and freedom in Jesus as proof of our ability to forsake our ancestral practices, your liberation was never part of their Christian gospel. When the Spanish Crown promised freedom in exchange for Christian conversion, fugitive slaves ran down from South Carolina to get some of that *old-time religion*. Slaveholders did not celebrate the saving of our souls. They feared we would learn of a Jesus whose mission is to liberate the captives and would, in turn, demand our full emancipation. By 1667, Virginia passed a law declaring that conversion did not change the status of a person from slave to free. Other colonies passed similar laws during the seventeenth and early eighteenth centuries.[3] *Whom the Son sets free is still a slave, indeed.*

It was not until widespread Protestant evangelicalism, which emphasized individual freedom, direct communication with God, and a defense of slavery, that the first large-scale conversion of enslaved men and women was brought about.[3] *This* is the gospel that Black folks were asked to hide in their hearts and reiterate in their churches by their oppressors. And it was the vision of Jesus as a master healer and liberator of the perils of the human condition that they feared most. They knew a *free* Jesus built a subversive faith and, ultimately, a wholesale rejection of their imposed identity as an accursed people. But if you never hear about *that* Jesus, can you ever receive Him?

> "So faith comes from what is heard, and what is heard comes through the word of Christ."
>
> —Romans 10:17 (NRSV)

The inevitable Black American inheritance (and, subsequently, the whole of the African diaspora affected by colonialism) of this Christian God, then, is our Blackness being named the most egregious sin. Our inheritance of this faith paints us a picture of God who ordained our enslavement and diminished our humanity. Hearing the gospel of a conquered and colonized Christ has told us that our enslavement—and all subsequent indignities of Blackness in America—is divinely orchestrated. We are left, then, with a faith practice whose core intention is to pray for the transfiguration of ourselves into whiteness by this imagining of God. Our connection to divinity has been and continues to be disrupted by the vain pursuit of embodying the acceptance and value of whiteness. Our God's image has *always* been both colonized and conquered.

This inherited theology—where we are passive participants helpless to the *perfecting* will of God—binds us to the demands of capitalism and its perpetual economy of desire for *more*. We are driven to work harder, faster, and longer in unnatural ways toward the pursuit of profit over happiness when acquiring material wealth is *also* seen as a sign of God's favor in this life and the next. Even in a religion whose sacred text insists that the love of money is the root of all evil, we've inherited a theological ethic that insists upon measuring our devotion, salvation, and holiness through the litmus of our capitalist success. This ethic suggests that "if one is graced by God, among the elect, one's ordinary pursuits will be coolly self-disciplined, restrained, non-hedonistic, and in that way amenable to capitalist requirements."[4]

Everyone reads themselves into the story as the hero. A white slave owner in the early colonies reading the Exodus text would see themselves as the Israelites resisting Egypt, the British. You know, even though they should probably see themselves as Egypt since they owned literal and not just politically figurative people. So by the time Whiteness™ gets to Jesus, it must ignore his entire life and focus on his last three days to have a Jesus that fits the requirements of subjugating a people. When they get to Jesus, they see suffering that can be amplified as an idyllic life for Black people. The only way they can do that is to ignore the work that Jesus did to free people. The faith that was forced on enslaved Africans rendered Jesus impotent in his work and magnificent in his suffering. This is how we inherit a Christianity that emphatically lands on a *Suffering Jesus*.

It's reducing life to the equivalent of a snapshot. It's like when a textbook features a picture of an enslaved foremother. What those Black people were in that photo at that time is the summation of their humanity: they were enslaved. We don't know what brought them joy, hope, or the love that kept them living through hell. They just become symbolic of a suffering period. That's what they do with Jesus. They take the moment when the state kills Him, and what follows that murder, and make it the most important thing about Him.

We are convinced that Christ's death liberated us from the onerous tenets of every law and Levitical code except those that maintain control over marginalized bodies. In a society where we are robbed of our communal resources through economic burden, and subsequently denied recourse for recovery, we seek wealth through morality. Scriptures meant to condemn pedophilia, ephebophilia, and child sex trafficking are cruelly twisted to condemn queer bodies. We are persuaded to trust that God is far more concerned with what we do *with* our bodies—sex, drinking, or modification—than with the systemic violence committed against this flesh. At the root of this self-sustained oppression is anti-Blackness, and the immersion of our theology in the fires of white supremacy teaches us of a God who rewards our self-loathing. We have been taught to give our breath over to empty prayers of deliverance from our innate human behaviors and for endurance to suffer through hegemonic evil.

What if we inherited a faith that focused on a *Serving Jesus* instead of glorifying the suffering as most divine? A Jesus who uses his patriarchal privilege to protect an accused adulterous woman in a social hierarchy that would've certainly killed her otherwise. What if our faith emphasizes a Jesus who makes room for *sexual others* in Matthew 19:11-12, even knowing that not everyone would accept this teaching? He says as much, beginning the message with, "Not everyone can accept this word," in verse 11. Those letters are in *red*, y'all, so I ain't making up the dialogue here.

We gain nothing from the wealth of moral superiority feigned through queer/trans antagonism, gendered violence, and sexual repression beyond the irrational sense that these actions will merit a "well done, thy good and faithful servant" on our judgment day. Yet, once this ethic becomes part of our enculturation, we are habituated into it regardless of our religious beliefs. Just as our ancestors' lives were traded and sold away by a few of our people on the shores of West Africa, imperialism continues its wicked work of making us participants in our oppression by rewarding our harm against one another in the name of Jesus.

The death penalty of perpetual enslavement is that even when our bodies are free, we remain disinherited when we do not receive what is rightfully ours through birthright. By romanticizing the power of suffering, we have been given a faith that will never free us *enough*. Our inherent Blackness is not a cause for a life of suffering for atonement.

Without the inheritance of the faiths of collective African ancestors, we lose the identity of what makes this brutal faith able to be redeemed from the hegemonic enemy. Romans 11:29 says, "For the gifts and calling of God are without repentance." Without a doubt, we—and I do mean all of us, white people—must believe and accept that *Blackness* is an unrepentant gift of God. Not in place of *other* lives but alongside them all. We are highly emotionally expressive and exceptionally creative. The musical composition of a *church sound* is so complex that it defies the laws of music theory. We have mastered tapping into the heart through chord structures *and* vocal intonations. We are loud, and we are light that is not well-hidden in a bushel. Hell, let's be real. We got that *Black cool*, and everybody and *they* mama want some of that shit too.

"Without repentance" means that God won't change Her mind about what She has called, so maybe it's time to revisit what God has called Blackness in that earlier text of terror, Genesis 9.

Let's assume that most of this story is correct. If we go with the story as presented, Noah only cursed Canaan in his drunken stupor. Holding the intended narrative of white supremacy requires it to assert itself as powerful enough to make a curse pass on through generations. But before Noah could open his mouth to curse Ham's son, God had already spent the top half of the chapter blessing Noah, his sons, *and their children*. As the saying goes, "Who Jah bless, no man can curse!" Despite using the words of some drunken man's wounded ego as justification for virulent anti-Blackness, God calls the children of Ham blessed. So even if we are the descendants of Ham, there is no rationalization for mishandling what God already blessed. And God's blessing of Blackness is not something She has changed her mind about.

When Black people adopt this faith in a *Suffering Christ*, we are (and have been for centuries) led to minimize Jesus's life and His work in exchange for amplifying His suffering, and that has, frankly, been to the detriment of Black people this entire time. Choosing to see Jesus as more than His suffering frailty is also calling Black folks to realize that what Jesus did was justice work. The humiliation of His death is not more important than the purpose of His living.

As the scripture notes, "For we do not fight against flesh and blood but against *powers and principalities*" (Ephesians 6:12 [NRSV]). There will never be enough antiracism education for people committed to ignoring the reality of the oppressed. In the work of liberation and justice, we are fighting something at the literal root of all things unholy, and it does not want to be uprooted at any cost. If the Christian faith is of any use to us today, it must understand that the last, suffering, undignified moments of Christ is not the *best* kind of faith a Serving Christ comes to offer us. And that's the kinda Jesus that strikes fear in the heart of supremacy.

· 6 ·

Will There Be One?

BECAUSE I AM A vocal critic of the Black Church and its culture, one would likely assume that I *hate* the church. Nothing could be further from the truth. One does not fight as hard or as intently as I do to preserve something they do not value. Working to deliver us collectively from the hands of white supremacist theology is a labor of love. It is born of my profound respect for the storied, sacred, cultural space that is the Black Church. Yet, our day of reckoning is here as the future of this cornerstone institution is looking *real* shaky. So consider this a *Come to Jesus* invitation of love rather than a rallying cry for execution.

> "The church, which should express a living, eternally growing, and eternally developing organism expressing the unity of men with God, can turn into a frozen, mechanical form."
>
> —JOHN S. POBEE, *TOWARD AN AFRICAN THEOLOGY* (1979)[1]

The benediction was always my favorite in all the moving parts of Sunday worship service. It signals the imminent close of the hours-long service and invites us to experience transformation. As we prepare to depart from sacred gatherings and reenter our daily lives, the benediction invokes God's blessings, protection, and guidance. Just before the benediction is the invitation to discipleship. It is a moment where we're invited to search our hearts for what healing we need. We're encouraged to check ourselves for unforgiveness, anger, and darkness. It is a moment of solemn introspection where we must search deeply to work out our soul salvation. Almost always, the pastor asks, "Will there be one" to answer the call. Now the call is coming from inside the house. If the church continues to lose its relevance, will there be one in our future?

Even as the world has run a marathon, the church remains reluctant to move its feet. The church chooses to excuse its toxic theology with the rationale that "God never changes." We call ourselves progressive when we "love the sinner and hate the sin" in response to constant attacks on queer lives. We worship the same God, but we squabble over theological interpretation and create new denominations of the Christian faith because of it. Our churches and congregations remain deeply split along color lines. On Sundays after the latest gendered, sexualized, or racially motivated act of violence, Christians frequently remain comfortably silent in their unaffected privileges while others are crushed under the weight of systemic oppression and injustice. While these things happened in plain sight, people are expected to uncritically engage a complacent church.

By 2050, the percentage of the US population attending church will be nearly half of what it was in 1990.[2] The focus of the conversation is my generation, millennials, the most secular in recent American memory. In 2015, only 27 percent of millennials attended religious services regularly.[2] Who can blame us? We've watched the world and its societies evolve at a mind-bending pace with awe while being asked to devote ourselves to an antiquated church. The majority of us—more than 85 percent—were raised Christian, and yet more than a third of us refuse to darken the door of any church now.[3] We attended children's church and Vacation Bible School. We registered for youth conferences and gave up our party weekends for church lock-ins. We lifted our voices and cried at the altar, repenting for everything we'd been convinced was sinful. We committed our lives, bodies, and souls to Christ to remain *set apart* from the world before we even knew ourselves. Our parents heeded the words of Proverbs 22:6, training us in the way that we should go. As we've grown older, we've felt no choice but to depart from a religious path that seemingly leads to a dead end.

Still, to imagine a future without the Black Church is akin to throwing out the baby with the bathwater. It is no secret that Black folks are more religious than the US population. Eighty-seven percent of Black folks describe themselves as a person of faith.[4] Yet, the echo of the exiting footsteps of millennials from the Black Church has grown from a mumble into a roar. From Conservative Baptist to Full Gospel, from the Church of God in Christ to Pentecostal Assemblies of the World, the Black Church is still a cornerstone of our lived experience, even for those who've left it behind.

Our exodus from these hallowed grounds is not out of misguided rebellion. We did not need our choirs replaced with highly produced, dimly-lit worship concert experiences. We weren't looking for pastors to be social media influencers. Our souls can't be fed by viral sound bites that amount to little more than motivational speaking in a preaching cadence. We desired deeper connections and conversations about God. For us, there is a nonnegotiable need to be deeply rooted and connected by shared experience. We desire leaders whose humanity authentically reflects our own. Far too many pastors are relying on the emotionalism of the charismatic church tradition that has fallen on ears that are unwilling to hear. We are not impressed with sermons held together by sexism, classism, and homophobia. We want tools for survival in a world that seems to hate us. We wanted an experience of God that made room for the whole self, and we didn't find that in your churches.

This search for God is why I reimagine the biblical text with intention. I challenge the theological frameworks that don't serve to liberate all Black folks. We need to see the sacredness of Black, queer, marginalized genders, disabled, and other lives often forced into the shadows. Being made in the image of God is not done with conditions of cisgender heteronormativity. We should see God reflected within these identities, not as things that cast us outside God's love. I fight to liberate our relationship to faith and spirituality because I believe rearticulating oppression in the name of biblical inerrancy is out of integrity with following Christ.

I believe our souls can be redeemed from the sin and shame of gatekeeping hegemony. I'm a witness through not only my decolonization but also that of my parents and the individuals and community I have served. I have not built my platform on being anti-church or dismantling the institution with no room to dream of what comes next. I, in fact, do not wish to see the Black Church dismantled but instead pray that she is transformed by the renewing of her mind beyond the marginalization of her people through queer antagonism, misogynoir, and upheld white supremacy. I desire a revolution that helps it thrive while empowering our community toward an experience of freedom in *every* way. Freedom that extends to our spirits, hearts, minds, and bodies. If Christ came that we might have life and have it abundantly, the church cannot continue to declare itself as His bride while actively sabotaging His purpose in showing up: to set the captives free. Abundance in bondage simply doesn't exist, and sprinkling oppressive theology with the blood of Jesus doesn't change that.

The Black Church is not an institution that I objectively experience or observe. It is not merely an ideological concept that I interrogate and intellectually critique. At the risk of superficial cliché, I am persuaded that we as people are the church itself. There is no more subjective experience than the vulnerability of spiritual care. This collective experience exists only by communal agreements of what we believe and how we ethically engage our faith and one another. To deeply examine and deconstruct those agreements is an act that must occur first within ourselves.

I do this work out of an unyielding love for an indisputable cultural institution and a passionate belief that it is worth saving for future generations. Stated plainly, if the church refuses to evolve to serve the needs of our people, it will inevitably be left to self-destruct.

> "Black memory is a form of disruption. It's a weapon not just because of efforts to erase it. But, also because it is precise. It is accurate. It is a catalogue [sic] of what we want to remember least."
>
> —Dr. Jenn M. Jackson, Associate Professor of Political Science (Syracuse University)[5]

For a significant portion of Black memory, the Black Church is a witness and cultural custodian of our collective experience. As an institution, it has served to, as Dr. Jackson names, "memorialize, archive, and witness the white supremacist, carceral violence of Anti-Blackness."[6] It is in our witness and public memory-making that we find an indelible tool of disruption. And, despite its current state, the Black Church has historically been a critical actor in the work of Black liberation.

It was out of the Black Church that the rebellions of Denmark Vesey, Nat Turner—both preachers—and Gabriel* were birthed. Even within religious indoctrination intended to justify the indefensible abuse, exploitation, and violence against Black bodies, there was a witness of a God on the side of the oppressed. Carceral violence told a narrative of a God who delighted in their subjugation as penance for the supposed moral failings of Blackness. Their witness birthed a religious culture that emphasized liberation from oppression. They found their liberation between the lines of inherited scriptures of Israelite deliverance in Egypt and imprinted indigenous African spiritual practices. And for the spooky saints who tremble in fear at the mention of African spirituality, make no mistake: without the retention of the rites and rituals of these practices, there is no *Black* Church.

Vesey, along with Gullah Jack, an East African priest, and other leaders of the newly formed African Methodist Episcopal church, planned a rebellion to manifest God's promise of deliverance in the lives of enslaved people. It was both Vesey's prayers grounded in liberation theology *and* Gullah Jack's conjure work that folks took hope in. In recorded testimony from the trial of the *Denmark Vesey Slave Conspiracy of 1822*, an enslaved person named Rolla said of Vesey's preaching in their weekly meetings: "He then read in the Bible where God commanded that all should be cut off, both men, women, and children, and he said, he believed, it was no sin for us to do so, for the Lord had commanded us to do it."[7] As history records, the rebellion failed due to exposure by enslaved folks who

---

* Gabriel is sometimes referred to using "Prosser" as an adapted surname from enslaver Thomas Henry Prosser, but historians say this is inaccurate.

revealed the plot to their masters about a month before its planned date. With the gift of freedom and hindsight, it is easy to feel enraged toward those who acquiesced to power. It is even easier to forget that we are products of our conditioning, and, as such, their decisions more likely reflected their survival instincts than their desires for freedom.

Nat Turner's rebellion teaches us that Black memory is also *prophetic*. Turner was born only one week before the execution of Gabriel, a Black abolitionist prosecuted for a failed rebellion. Like our cultural tradition of passing children over caskets at a burial site to imbue them with the best qualities of the newest ancestor, Turner's birth in this time foreshadows his life to come. His preternatural knowledge and other signs marked him as a prophet by his people at a young age. It is said that Turner had three visions that divined how to carry out what would eventually be a blood-drenched act of resistance. He describes his final vision: "I heard a loud noise in the heavens, and the Spirit instantly appeared to me and said the Serpent was loosened, and Christ laid down the yoke he had borne for the sins of men, and that I should take it on and fight against the Serpent, for the time was fast approaching when the first should be last, and the last should be first . . . And by signs in the heavens that it would be made known to me when I should commence the great work, and until the first sign appeared I should conceal it from the knowledge of men; and on the appearance of the sign, I should arise and prepare myself and slay my enemies with their own weapons."[8]

While neither Turner nor his comrades made it out of the rebellion alive, they struck fear deep in the hearts of slaveholders and their accomplices that perhaps their *properties* were not so docile, meek, or mild. These rebellions are an unequivocal subversion of supremacist imaginings of God. Undoubtedly, these Black memories defined the church not only as a site of freedom, but as one that is self-aware of its power to redefine social narratives, appropriately redirect accountability, and identify harm that might otherwise be cloaked by stature or position.[5]

The Black Church decries biblical *texts of terror*[9] that rationalize the dehumanization of Blackness, from enslavement to Jim Crow and through US presidents who sow racial and ethnic discord. We've condemned and rebuked anti-Blackness from the pulpit without feeling conflicted with God's word. Black preachers have been at the center of every "event that captures people's experiences and draws them out from their isolation into a collective force with the power to transform conditions."[10] From Rev. Dr. Martin Luther King's *Mountaintop* to Rev. Dr. William J. Barber's Poor People's Campaign and the scathing rebuke of Bishop Talbert Swan's tweets in between, the Black memory of God as a liberator has remained with us. Despite texts like "slaves, obey your masters," we've *been* willing to do the work to excavate passages for nuance, culture, and historical context. Our unwillingness to make the cross a site of liberation for folks whose marginalizations intersect at gender and sexuality is a deliberate choice. It will ultimately ring as the death knell for the church if we do not course correct.

This tradition of God as a liberator of the oppressed has made the church what scholar-activist Keeanga-Yamahtta Taylor describes as a catalytic *movement actor*. These change agents provide a counter-narrative that raises the issues faced by those whose experiences would otherwise be forced into the shadows.[5] The absence of revolutionary resistance from the pulpit has only deepened the fissure in our relationship. There is a longing to see the church of the civil rights and Black Power movements, which was a church that was not afraid to position itself at the front lines to fight against systemic oppression. Instead, we are left with a church that runs on the residue of its glory years as the center of the Black community, a reality that couldn't be further from our present truth.

Our expanded access to the global lives of others has made us more politically aware than ever. We seek refuge in our churches and are only met with antics that tickle our emotions. We're disinterested in seeing white supremacy reinforced in the pulpit. We desire to be equipped to take on a society that hates us, and we need to be told more than "just pray about it." Hellfire and brimstone sermons aren't moving us to join the ranks of your membership rosters. Witnessing state-sanctioned murders at the hands of law enforcement coupled with a political regime that deepens our marginalization daily is enough hell in itself.

Church leaders and rabidly devoted adherents tend to blame its hemorrhaging membership on shifting cultural norms. Like many of them, mandatory church attendance is a dominant feature of my religious childhood experience. I was *raised* in the church, and what I witnessed in the pew *then* is precisely why I avoid the pew *now*. I saw pleas for God's deliverance from impoverishment go unanswered. Not because God refused to meet the need but out of the church's unwillingness to be a vessel. I've witnessed people seeking help from their church homes turned away in times of financial crisis because of their *tithing* record. I've watched babies denied the christening rites because of the parents' marital status. My witness of a church that prioritized the politics of the platform over the needs of the people has been enough to drive *me* out.

As a collective, the church has been a poor representation of the transformative power of salvation. We see Christian women vacant of any semblance of individuality, so insecure in their personhood in pursuit of the vain glory of paternalistic virtuosity. We see Christian men who abuse their power, partners, and children despite their profession of faith. We see pastors, deacons, and trustees use their positions to coerce some and assault others simply to satisfy their uncontrolled lust. We see folks who profess Christ and deny the rights and liberties of others in the same breath. What remains reflects a Christ who has certainly not done *enough*. Despite zealous devotion, colonized Christian values haven't changed Christian lives—or hearts.[11]

We're exiting our congregations because we don't see *ourselves*. Our sanctuaries are adorned with depictions of saints and a savior whose skin doesn't look like ours. Our leaders are attempting to scapegoat racism as an issue of sin rather than skin. The church's preference for respectability over discipleship has led to an edging out at the cross for those who fall short of Christian exceptionalism. Respectable Christian Politics (RCP) is a set of requirements where sin must fall within respectable limits to be eligible for salvation and the right hand of fellowship within our churches. RCP has defined our acceptable dress code, style of worship, and even which sins we confess and address. RCP reinforces the myth that Christian exceptionalism is the cure for anti-Blackness. It is not by accident that evangelical Christianity traditionally associates black with death, sin, and evil, while white is associated with purity, innocence, and holiness. It is not simply a "difference of opinion" when opponents argue against seeing Jesus through the lens of Black lived experience. As whiteness continues to be prized as the ultimate marker of civility, the desire to gain favor in the sight of White Gaze will remain—even in the faith.

We can't do homophobia, misogyny, classism, and white supremacy thinly veiled as Christian doctrine. We are too educated to overlook the glaring injustice of the world and reinforced oppressions in the church. We recognize that at the root of a fascist problem is a *religious* problem. We're cringing at the *amen club* preachers have built on the backs of LGBTQIA+ people. We wince at the outdated sexist remarks casually tossed from the pulpit. We're not coming to church to socially climb, yet we've been shown that we must adopt an anti-them mentality to fit in with fellow parishioners. We craved the divine and became disillusioned instead.

Each day, we grapple with the relentless onslaught of fear and anguish. We sought refuge in your sanctuaries from the treacherous waters of supremacy that tried to drown us. We came to your altars longing for something so profound and vital that we would willingly endure torment to attain it. In the churches we have encountered, Christianity appears devoid of transformative power. We are only offered performative practices that edge us out. A faith that proffers nothing more than trinkets of false comfort at best and delusion at worst.

We enter your sanctuaries in a delicate dance of anticipation, our souls parched and breath bated for even a fleeting experience of spiritual nourishment. As much as we needed Her to be there, we did not find God. Instead, we saw cheap replicas of systemic oppression committed in Jesus's name in country clubs masquerading as churches. To ignore the message our absence is sending will only accelerate the church's course toward becoming a historical relic. We are not a generation lost; your churches have simply not made themselves a home to be found.

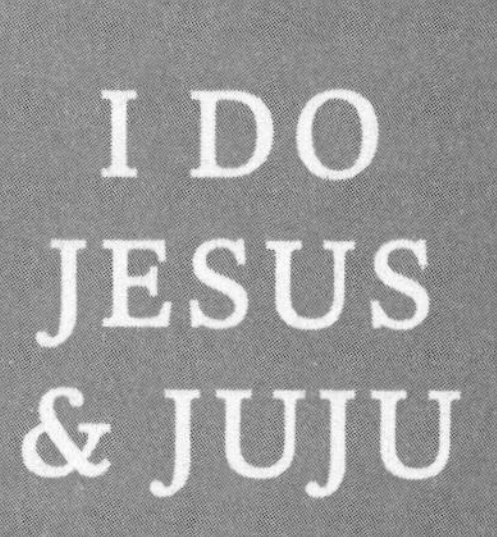

I DO JESUS & JUJU

Open Their Eyes

2 Kings 6:17
Has always been the scene
So, I saw you coming
Before you knew what the plan was.
Pitch forks, fires, and screams don't scare me.
I've been cursed with truth and vision my whole life.
Just because you can't see
Won't see
Refuse to see
Does not mean I'm obligated to go blind.

—Valerie B

• 7 •

"The Enemy Is in the House Tonight"

I KNEW EXACTLY WHAT *I was doing when I decided to pay a surprise visit to my former church home after my unceremonious dismissal more than five years before. I had as much to prove to myself as I needed to prove to them by stepping into that sanctuary. I'd loved my pastors in earnest since childhood, and they'd thrown that love back on my face with added humiliation and self-doubt. If I couldn't get full atonement for their sins against me, I sure as hell would take the satisfaction of making them as uncomfortable as possible.*

Church membership is something you gain either by inheritance or you're recruited by invitation—there is no in-between. The recruitment cycle is a subtle, insidious one. It begins with cultivating trust and a sense of community, an oasis for the spiritually wounded, and draws you into the church's charismatic orbit. The first encounter with the church sweetly entices the potential new member. The warmth of welcoming smiles and offers of kindness from everyone you meet disarms your defenses. The invitation to the community from the visitor acknowledgment to the altar call erases all doubts of apocryphal niceties. As far as first impressions go, almost no institution comes close to the church that poses itself as a friendly, supportive community generously offering a sense of purpose and belonging to those who join.

A pastor can make or break the success of recruitment. Nothing quite like a charismatic preacher who exudes confident authority can inspire devoted obedience in their followers that drives them to witness the name of their *(wo)man of God* to anyone willing to listen. Mama's—and subsequently, my—recruitment process began with an invitation to attend this amazing new church from her friend's current flavor of the month in a string of suitors. The sanctuary, situated between a defunct insurance office and dry cleaners on the main street of a sleepy suburb, bellowed with a sound fit for an audience ten times its occupied size. A few dozen congregants ranging in age filled the small but tidy space with joyful noise, well in the swing of praise and worship by the time we arrived. Intrigued but warm gazes fell on us as we moved to our seats, quickly assembling ourselves to fall into the groove of service. Unlike their larger counterparts, there is no hiding in intimate spaces like this.

There is an immediate recognition of your status as an outsider concealed beneath those small smiles and curious gazes. Members of the church immediately profile you for their safety and your potential goodness of fit. They'll pull you into warm embraces and lull you into feelings of connectedness as cheerful words of welcome brush past your ears, all the while assessing you by a rubric understood only by those enculturated in the politics of the church. We must've passed that first test with flying colors since we'd been invited to stay for family dinner and a second *evening* service by the benediction. I don't know if Mama was completely sold; in fact, I'd argue that she likely wasn't. But like any good recruiter, a charismatic leader is trained to overcome objections.

I was nine years old the summer I witnessed my first exorcism in that storefront church I'd call my *church home* for the next five years.

The evening service went much like the first: spirited musical praise, money collection, a fiery sermon, and an altar call. Only a few faces had changed since the morning crowd, but among them was the possessed soul who'd become etched in my memory for a lifetime. She was rather unremarkable physically, looking nothing like the depictions of those needing exorcism from the horror films I'd watched. Yet when the pastor called her out during his prophetic move—the portion of religious services where supernatural messages are given to individuals through a conduit—he declared to her that he recognized her spirit before informing the congregation that this was an unclean entity among us.

Exorcism rituals are nothing like the ones of visual media's colorful imagination—at least not my experience of it. The harsh brightness of halogen lights filled the sanctuary instead of candlelit darkness. Palms slicked with anointing oil replaced the smoky incense, and the gathered congregants' murmuring prayers took the place of invocations in dead languages. Despite the jarring, perhaps even violent, rites of exorcism, we were not excluded as children. Instead, we were invited to bear witness, as part of the continued training of children in the *righteous* way we ought to go.

As the pastor began to speak to the evil indwelling, I remember the woman started to wryly laugh while her body moved as if she were in a drunken stupor. The people prayed harder, and the prophet worked determinedly to call the spirit subject to the power of God. While we tarried for the Holy Ghost to fall and deliver us from evil, the intensity of the ritual reached a fevered pitch. The woman's laughter turned to wailing tears when the prophet spoke in tongues. Before I knew it, her diminutive body was doubled over before collapsing onto all fours and violently vomiting on the floor—a declarative victory that the demonic spirit within her had been expelled. The sanctuary erupted into exuberant praise, basking in the wonder of the power of God to victoriously triumph over evil once more.

While she lay on the floor, utterly exhausted from the ordeal, the pastor opened the doors of the church for discipleship. I never saw that woman again, but her deliverance became our initiation rite, completing the recruitment cycle from candidate to member. Although one might think that people who casually dispossess presumably malevolent spirits from the body would be amenable to ritual magick, this was only the beginning of my understanding of the evangelical rebranding of ritual work as *gifts of the Spirit* for themselves and *witchcraft* for everyone else.

Coming into the fold of a ministry is a courting process complete with all the infatuation and euphoria of any newly minted relationship during its honeymoon phase. You're adopted into the community and given new honorifics of *sister* or *brother* added to your name in all conversations. The instructional curriculum of new members' classes has been perfectly designed to explain the rules of engagement for the beliefs and ideologies you're now expected to uphold as neophyte church family members. This process is the same regardless of the congregation size and is essential to the function and growth of any ministry.

Critics of the Black Church often focus their ire on the embattled finances of megachurches. Storefront churches move surreptitiously under their uncritical eye. While leaders of those 2,000+ seat auditoriums are interrogated for their failed wealth redistribution within our communities, others occupy the empty units of squalid office buildings, strip malls, and hotel conference rooms, positioning themselves as the righteous alternative to the corrupted greed of their mega-sized counterparts. The palpable distrust of megachurches is a goldmine for the storefront church recruitment strategy. To those seeking intimate connection with God in earnest, these small congregations with easy access to pastoral care and connection make a strong appeal. As intimacy increases and vulnerability deepens, the church becomes, without notice, the central focus of their life. With childlike impressionability, sincere adherents are quickly caught up in the esotericism of pastors with unbridled authority and little accountability. The church's ideology becomes all-encompassing, permeating every aspect of the members' lives. The psychological manipulation most feared at the hands of deep-pocketed, highly visible preachers is most alive within the churches next door to the laundromat and discount store in the plaza a couple of streets over.

The breaking of my sense of self to ensure my loyalty and commitment to God and my new church home was a slow but steady process. I was quickly put to work in the ministry, joining the dance team and youth choir simultaneously, which unsurprisingly was rostered by the same children in each group. A textbook extrovert, I formed friendships quickly with the other children, including the daughter of my husband-and-wife pastoral team with whom I developed a deep bond.

Churches are not impervious to hierarchies of power, and learning its distinct social pecking order is a critical lesson in matriculation of church culture. The first family—the pastor, along with their spouse and children—lead the pack, and their importance is second only to God. Social power descends to associate pastors, ministerial staff, musicians who are either dispensable or invaluable depending on the impact of the church's music ministry, and then everyone else. Successful social mountaineering depends on one's ability to prove their utility in raising the status and visibility of those at the top. It can be more cutthroat than comparable secular groups. The social status of a PK may be inherited, but it is also complicated. We must be friendly with and show kindness to all, but our selection of those who make up our inner circle has far-reaching consequences. Our closest friends benefit from our social capital but must also carry the burden and duty of protecting our personal and familial image. Becoming part of our inner sanctum comes with the expectation that we can trust you with our humanity beyond the hallowed hallways of our church—and there is hell to pay when the trust is broken.

That first summer in my childhood church home brought with it a rocketed ascension through the social ranks for me and Mama, with her becoming the church administrator and my firmly established *best friend* ranking with my pastor's eldest daughter. Little did we know we'd spend the next several years paying the cost of these coveted positions.

> "How does one group subjugate another group of people? You subjugate a people by telling them that their science is superstition, their faith is heresy, and their wisdom is make believe."
>
> —Amos Bludso (as portrayed by Blair Underwood), *Bad Hair*[1]

I was thirteen the year I learned that I was a seer—possessing the gift of supernatural insight for future prediction. In church, it is the gift of prophecy, but when used in any other way, it is quickly demonized as witchcraft. This belief complicated my relationship with my gift before it even began. After almost five years, the efficacy of the rose-tinted-glass perspective we had of our church home was starting to wane. Our positions felt less covetous and more cumbersome, burdened by a myriad of secrets and contradictions we were required to hold in silence. Mama and I dedicated much of our social lives exclusively to the church and particularly the protection of the first family in our respective roles.

My friendship with ol' girl was rockier than ever, complicated by the emotional volley of my burgeoning teenage girlhood and several new girls vying for my position at her side. Intoxicated by power, her egocentrism soon outpaced our mutual loyalty and left us at odds. When my nascent prophetic dreams began to form visions of my estranged best friend being with child, my indoctrination quickly shut them down as evidence of the occult attempting to corrupt my soul. For me, these dreams depicted the unspeakable and unfathomable. We were *good girls*, raised upright. I believed that we were the kind of girls who would never have sex outside of marriage and especially not have irrefutable evidence of our sin against God through an unplanned pregnancy. I rebuked my dreams, begging God to protect my mind from malignant forces in the vulnerability of my sleep. Instead, my dreaming intensified and quickly blurred the lines between my waking life and the one formed by the interconnected regions of my brain.

As if unwilling to allow me to dismiss the dreams as meaningless, I began to see just enough mimicry of scenes from my dreams within my waking life to confirm that these experiences were not figments of my imagination. When I finally told my mom of these recurring dreams, I'd learned that I'd not been dreaming alone. Mama's dreams of my bestie's belly swollen with life were often in sync with my own, and we found that our visions were sometimes identical once we compared our notes. Despite our aggrieved relationship, I was deeply worried about the well-being of my friend, whom I perceived as being on the cusp of an irreparable life change.

The Sunday that changed everything began as any ordinary Sunday did at that point—estranged bestie in position leading praise and worship and me seated in the congregation. Her countenance was uncharacteristically nervous for someone who found their home in the spotlight behind a microphone. She spent most of the time fidgeting anxiously, casting furtive glances between her mother and sister. The others were too caught up in the theater of worship to notice, but I found it challenging to focus on anything but the unease etched on her face. Despite—or maybe because of—my sex-negative enculturation, I learned early how to intuit the telltale signs of sexual activity and pregnancy. For better or worse, it is almost a perfect science.

As we fell into the full swing of service, I studied her carefully, and my suspicions were all but confirmed when the intentionally shapeless dress formed itself around an unmistakably round belly for a few moments. Fractal images of my previous dreams flooded into the forefront of my mind, aligning themselves to affirm a narrative I knew but wished was untrue. My empathy for her melted every feeling of resentment I held for her. That evening, long after service ended and I'd had time to contemplate my approach, I called my friend to offer my help. I asked first if she thought she might be pregnant, to which she provided an inconclusive answer of, "It doesn't matter at this point." After assuring her of the sincerity of my offers for help, our brief call ended. Two hours passed before *her* mama called *my* mama to chastise us *both* for the mere suggested possibility that *her* daughter might be pregnant.

Though Mama defended my good intentions throughout that call, the following day, Mama and I were unceremoniously dismissed from the church we'd given so much of ourselves to for years. We'd committed the cardinal sin of seeing more than we should've and knowing enough to shatter the carefully built public illusion they presented. Our departure became a scarlet letter marking us as lepers in a community we were once believed to be invariable members of. In the fallout, we'd soon find a new home under the leadership of another pastor who'd passed through our former church home before being driven out too. While that community experience was far less traumatic, it did little to mend the severance between my supernatural gifting and my willingness to *see* anything not tangibly established.

My father's death catapulted me into the confrontation of self I'd repressed for over a decade. By that point, my clairvoyance expanded to clairaudience, and I no longer needed dreams for future prediction. The night Daddy died, I heard Spirit gently ask, "Do you remember your dad's funeral plans?" I couldn't afford the toll on my mental health to believe that I was actively foreshadowing his death when I so faithfully believed in his miraculous healing. He'd spent twenty years preparing me for his inevitable demise, but I never questioned my knowledge of his final wishes during one of his bouts of illness. The voice was one I'd heard for years but put little stock into as I determined the course of my life. As far as I was concerned, listening to that voice once had done more harm than good, and my world was better off relying on what I could prove. As someone with profound intuitive gifting, I earnestly believe I knew what I didn't want to know: I was losing my Daddy that night and was helpless to intervene. My denial allowed small protection for my fragile psyche in grief, but it was only a reprieve. It was not just church hurt that I needed to work through, but I needed to reclaim and fully integrate *all* facets of myself that I'd repressed as dangerous spiritual entities seeking whom they may devour.

Our willingness to give over our power to create, shift, and materialize liberated realities in Jesus's name is the legacy of whitewashed theologies promoted as the gospel. Our churches embody theological tenets that demonize honoring the ancestors we *know* have our best interests at heart while teaching us to instead call on the name of Jesus in times of peril, summoning the power of a savior whose physical image is identical to the arbiters of the perilous fates from which we seek salvation. Our Christian faith hinges on worshiping a common master ancestor in Jesus, so to demonize ancestral veneration of our bloodlines is *wild*.

It is not the disembodied name of Jesus that saved us from the inhumane indignities of enslavement and subsequent colonization across the diaspora. The rites and rituals of those before us and the workings we so carelessly call witchcraft ensured our survival. Those prayers of the righteous became the invocations that availed against the unceasing evils of hegemony. Without a doubt, God can only see me in my fullness through the complete integration of *all* the spiritual practices imbued within my lineage that allow my bloodlines to survive multiple atrocities to get me here. I am no longer willing to live in ways that have a form of godliness but actively deny the power within out of fear and poor understanding of how our desperation for salvation is weaponized against us.

The night I returned to my childhood church—at the invitation of a current member—after the dust of our dismissal had long since settled, my recovery was such that I was far more comfortable in my self-awareness. I hadn't actively started my religious decolonization, but I no longer cared that I was a walking contradiction to the beliefs that once shaped the foundations of my faith. The church had moved from the town square to its freestanding formal edifice. Stepping inside quickly transported me back to that first Sunday at nine years old. For all their faults, my childhood pastors always maintained a bomb-ass music ministry, and this first night of revival was no exception. The crowd was bigger now, but among them was a sea of familiar faces and trepid smiles, unsure if the crimson stain of my previous censure remained. Children I'd once held as lap babies now made up the new generation of young adults, finding their places within the social order. My former bestie and her siblings occupied their usual places behind their mother, the co-pastor and bishop's wife, leading praise and worship. Noticeably absent was a small child calling ol' girl mama, and, without evidence to the contrary, it was as if nothing ever happened. Her cryptic reply to my assistive offers that night had a sudden new clarity in its intended meaning.

Mama and I took our seats and fell in step with the rest of the congregation just like the first time. I don't know what reception I expected walking in, but I was prepared for anything. As the high-energy song came to its close, my former pastor began her transitioning exhortation to lead us into the next song. As she spoke about the promises of God and protection from harm, her eyes scanned the room before locking glances between Mama and me. Without breaking her gaze on me, she declared to the congregation that "the enemy is in the house tonight" before beginning the opening notes of a victorious war cry. It was an open rebuke—a soft exorcism, if you will—but this time, I was deemed as the unclean spirit. When I was a child, I spoke as a child with due deference and respect. But as a grown-ass woman with autonomy and disillusioned regard for self-aggrandized pastors, I laughed at her rattled discomfort, grabbed my purse, and left the sanctuary. *Mission accomplished.*

· 8 ·

If Jesus Don't Fix It, the Hoodoo Lady Will

ONE OF MY FAVORITE incantations in church is when we call the roll of Jesus. When we name Him as *Mary's baby*, we demonstrate familial belonging in a distinctly Black way. We describe Jesus as the *lily of the valley* or the *bright and morning star.* Where Jesus is a *waymaker* and *miracle worker*, our minds flood with memories of Jesus as a *promise keeper* and *wonder in our souls.* It is a distinct invocation of Spirit like none other.

Witchcraft is the practice of connecting with energies, spirits, or forces beyond the ordinary realm of existence to use those supernatural forces for various purposes. Despite claims to the contrary, these acts are undeniably present within the distinct Black articulation of Christian theology. The best conjure work I ever learned is from my lifelong church attendance. The most masterful root workers I've met have often been in the pulpits I sat under. Declaring these acts as being "*for evil*" is merely *churched* folks playing semantics.

While reading this, cognitive dissonance from years of sermons about witchcraft may trigger some defense mechanisms. It's easy to overlook the practices differentiating the Black Church experience in the mire of the supremacist theology uplifted in our sanctuaries. We made ancestral veneration more palatable through the beatification of saints. We're comfortable calling on the God of Abraham, Isaac, and Jacob but fear the invocation of the names of our ancestors. We worship the death and resurrection of Jesus, but calling on the intercessory prayers of an ascended grandparent is where we draw the line of necromancy. We've eschewed spiritual baths yet carry ourselves to the baptismal waters as a sacrament of initiation into the faith. We give tithes, sacrifice ourselves, and lay written prayer requests at the church altar but have demonized altars built for ancestors. And every Easter and First Sunday, we engage in a blood ritual of communion to unify ourselves with Christ while preaching against crystals and smoke smudging.

Our emotionally charged worship services invite spiritual energy and *entities* into our midst. We've perfected services that maximize our collective power to invoke spiritual *quickening*. We know the scripting needed to summon the Holy Spirit. We can provoke a transformative encounter with a renewed passion for worship, prayer, and service to God. The overwhelming joy, surges of energy, physical sensations, speaking in tongues, and prophetic utterances are unmistakable signs of the Holy Spirit's presence.

When the drums start talking through the rhythmic pulse of shouting music, our strongest ties to the ways of old are on display. What we call "catching the Holy Ghost" is little more than retaining the West African Ring Shout. Our enslaved ancestors placed their cultural identity, preserved their traditions, and expressed their spirituality in the face of oppressive conditions in this practice. Shouting provides a space for emotional release, healing, and seeking divine intervention. It is a powerful, palpable experience that creates a spiritual connection with ancestors, spirits, and the divine.

By definition, it still resembles the experiences and practices we often assign to witchcraft.

> The mere fact that a stance is adopted by an avowed Christian does not make it authentically Christian. Anything authentically Christian has to be supported either in detail or in spirit by the basic sources and tenets of the Christian faith. Anything authentically African has to be supported by proverbs, myths, songs, lyrics, rites, customs, and such [as the] primary sources of African ethos. Faith is the faith of a historical community with all its trappings. Faith is not static because no community is static.
>
> —John S. Pobee, Ghanaian theologian and former Vicar General of the Anglican Diocese of Accra, Ghana

I've casually engaged in rituals and spell work for my entire Black life, although I never heard it called that. We did ritualistic cleaning of every corner, counter, and item of clothing before the clock struck midnight of a new year to rid ourselves of the departing year's energy. After shouting, praying, and decreeing during Watch Night, New Year's dinners were never served without a side of greens for money, black-eyed peas for luck, and hot buttered cornbread for gold. It is a prosperity ritual, but as *good Christians*, we saw it merely as a *family tradition*. We believed that placing a hat on a bed would cause a household death, and sweeping someone's feet required the uncrossing work of spitting on the broom. We perform protection spells in every new space we call home. We anoint doorposts with oil, sweep floors with salt, and pray invocations of protective energy in Jesus's name. We attend family dinners with plates for empty seats and ancestor altars hiding in plain sight on fireplace mantles, coffee tables, and well-loved hallway walls.

Our tendency to label what we do not immediately understand as demonic speaks to a larger issue of supremacist theology taking root in Black faith traditions. I've spent years witnessing carefully formulated prayers, intentionally chosen scriptures, and specific verbal incantations intended to deliver specific outcomes, which holds the same intent as spell casting. If we need deliverance, we engage in the *laying of hands* to channel energy where we need it most. We believe that the Holy Spirit's power is transmitted through touch, bringing us physical, emotional, or spiritual healing. Hell, I don't even cook with Pompeian brand oil to this *day* because of my strict association with consecrated anointing oil. Where many see a bottle of pressed olives, I see the base for the sacred oil described in Exodus 30:22-25. There is little difference between a biblical formulary of olive oil infused with myrrh, cinnamon, calamus, and cassia as sacred anointing oil and a condition oil created with the same intention by a root worker aside from our indoctrination of suspicion for the latter.

The Black Christian tradition only exists because of the African cosmology through which it is both birthed and syncretized, which makes it inextricably linked. Our ancestors did not adopt this faith *until* they could marry it to the inherited spiritual practices of those who came before them. The sanitizing of those cosmological practices by different names—how spirit possession becomes *catching the Holy Ghost*—doesn't change the practices themselves or the divine source that empowers them. The only difference in how that source is called good or evil is who benefits from our disinheritance of fully knowing *ourselves*.

Reclamation requires the decolonization of spiritual work. By reframing the innate power of creation, we can see both practices of ritual and divination as the gift of being created in the image of God. What we call things matters. It is why the church will call my gift of future casting *prophetic* within its walls but *witchcraft* outside of them. If the casting of lots for divination is *sanctified* by its presence in both the Old and New Testaments, why is casting cowrie shells (Ifá) or diloggun (Lucumí) *demonic*? Only supremacist theology could drive us to juxtapose divine power as good or evil simply by what we call the work being performed. It is extremely *white* of us to position Christianity as the only valid path to access divinity.

The most extraordinary spellwork I witnessed in church is the divination ritual of prophecy. In the sweltering summer evenings of annual revivals, the air thickened with anticipation and the scent of souls yearned to be set free. The preparation for this ritual was always evident to me. I learned how to make myself invisible during the *prophetic move* by silencing my thoughts. I never enjoyed the absence of privacy that came with prophecy. Although some would whisper in the ear of the recipient, most messages were delivered in witness of the gathered public. Yet for the many who came for a move of God, there was palpable vulnerability and desire to be *called out* by the prophet.

The time of prophecy is usually placed after the sermon and just before the invitation to discipleship. Riding the high energy from the sermonic close, congregational voices echo and mingle, rising like a chorus of spirits unleashed. The prophet steps forth with an otherworldly grace that reaches into the depths of our weary hearts. The ritual begins in the physical, speaking prayers that submit their bodies as willing vessels for the divine. They start to speak in tongues, their words an ancient language dancing upon the air and unlocking the heavens before us. Spirits open, caught in a whirlwind of faith and ecstasy, carried away on the wings of the Holy Ghost.

In this sacred space, time loses all meaning. Worldly matters become insignificant in those hallowed moments as we surrender to the Spirit, bound by a shared experience of grace and redemption. The prophetic word proclaims the promises *and* judgment of God. Every syllable falls like rain on parched earth. It offers solace in a world that often forsakes us, and we drink it all in, thirsty for hope and deliverance. Healings unfold before our eyes, bodies convulsing with the release of pain and suffering. Demons are cast out, their power broken by the name of Jesus. When the last shout subsides and the final "Amen" is spoken, the air crackles with the energy of miracles. We've bathed ourselves in the glory of the divine.

I've conversed with Lucumí practitioners who've shared accounts so strikingly familiar that I effortlessly juxtaposed them with my own Christian encounters. The *misa* preceding priesthood initiation, wherein both Spirit and ancestors are invoked, mirrors my pursuit of ancestral blessings during crucial decisions. The *dia del Itá*, where initiates grasp their lifelong obligations by learning their strengths, weaknesses, and taboos, reflects my experiences of prophetic warnings. In the ritual of *rompimiento*, where the initiate is led to a river, divested of garments, and cleansed in its purifying waters, I discern the intention of water baptism, the ritual of purification and rebirth within my Christian tradition.

Obviously, we did not retain *all* of our respective Africanaity throughout the enslavement experience, nor should it be argued that we needed to.[1] Yet, what remains is self-evident in blending the beliefs we come from and those we picked up *in Jesus's name* along the way. Christian syncretism with West African religious traditions continues to thrive in our sanctuaries. It is where shouting, tarrying, and the utterance of unknown tongues become our communion with the divine. By the wisdom of Romans 4:17, we speak with unwavering faith, breathing life into the yet unseen realms to manifest our desires. With every breath, we summon forth resolute power, invoking the name of a crucified savior whose power is triumphantly resurrected within our collective consciousness every time we call His name.

In the depths of the Black Christian experience, our lives have long been steeped in rituals that, were they given any other label, our theological doctrines would promptly scorn as witchcraft. Ain't it worth questioning why we redefine the spirit *catchin'*, life-in-the-tongue *speakin'*, things unseen *seein' Blackity Black* spirituality we've always been doing as *evil*?

> African culture, for its part, has also been influenced by both European culture and Christianity. The long and short of the story is that the problem is in part to be able to distinguish genuine and nonnegotiable elements of Christianity from European culture, and to distinguish authentic Africaness from phony Africaness.
>
> —JOHN S. POBEE, *TOWARD AN AFRICAN THEOLOGY* (1979)[2]

From our first interactions, we've been taught to regard white Western culture and the nonnegotiable articles of the Christian faith as one and the same. Supremacist authoritarianism made its cultural norms theologically significant while demonizing Blackness as an inferior *other*. In the early days of conversion, drumming and libations were shunned in Christian meetings due to their association with traditional Nigerian and Ghanaian religious rites. When proposing the bishopric appointment of Rev. Samuel Ajayi Crowther of Nigeria to the Christian Missionary Society, the European missionaries *in* Nigeria vehemently rejected it. In reply to the letter from the secretary of the Christian Missionary Society, the missionary says, "We are allowed to teach and preach the Gospel . . . because God gives us influence as Europeans among them. But if they hear that a Black man is our master, they will question our respectability."[3] Neither the Bible nor the early church appeal to race as it concerns qualifications of the office of bishop, but imperialism is still *nasty* work. While Black-led congregations are now standard, what image of the cross do we bear?

Christianity did not reach West African shores or its *descendants* on the soil of America without the ethnocentric views of those who evangelized it. The condescending attitudes of mission work often cast Africans as "uncivilized" or "heathen" and believed it was their duty to "civilize" and convert them to Christianity. This mindset often led to a disregard for African cultures, practices, and traditions and a tendency to impose European values and norms. People who, before the arrival of white men, "knew how to build houses, govern empires, erect cities, cultivate fields, mine for metals, weave cotton, [and] forge steel"[4] were still classified as incorrigible souls sitting in darkness. *Darkness*, as described here, is not about lacking spiritual knowledge, and we ought to stop pretending otherwise. Accounts from missionaries about the unconquerable, barbaric souls of West Africans from darkness are not biblical revelation. This metaphorical darkness has always been an indictment of Blackness that has not yielded its autonomy to white authority.

Before it meets African traditional religion, Christianity reaches us, having already been syncretized by the cultures it has passed through to get here. Pobee agrees: "Christianity, as it came to West Africa, is a composite of the teachings of Jesus, Semitic (Jewish) culture, Greco-Roman culture, and European culture."[2] The argument has never truly been about indigenous African beliefs versus Christianity but the uplift of *Eurocentric* culture at the expense of our own as necessary for Christian conversion. Christian theology is a lot like the game of telephone: the intent of the original message loses quality as it passes through the filter of cultural influence.

By the time Christianity moved from Europe to Africa in the fifteenth century, it was redressed in distinct Eurocentrism. Colonized Christianity is insidious in its level of genius. It so easily convinces us that our salvation is in the erasure of our identity. The *Tabula rasa* doctrine suggests that nothing in the African spiritual culture can be redeemed and completely destroyed before *proper* Christian conversion can occur. Now, centuries later, we still struggle to discern the will of God from the idolatrous god of Western ideology.

Speaking of confusion, remember when Pastor Paula White popped out as a feral Trump supporter after building her career on the backs of Black congregations? Let me tell you a crazy story.

Back in 2000, Bishop T. D. Jakes legitimized Paula White as a "good white" pastor. She spoke at his Woman Thou Art Loosed conference and skyrocketed within the Black Pentecostal church for nearly two decades. Paula and her ex-husband Bishop Randy White started Without Walls International Church in 1991, and let me tell you, they were living *large*. Thanks to their mostly Black audiences and congregations, they were bringing in millions of dollars from their church and media ventures. We're talking $40 million for the church in 2006 alone! And Paula's media ministry, Paula White Ministries? That was raking in like $50K-$80K weekly. But here's the kicker: fast forward ten years, and guess who pops up on our TV screens? None other than Paula White herself giving an invocation for none other than Donald J. Trump.

We might've been less offended if she hadn't stood on our necks to live out her dream of proximal political influence. Alas, she only carried on a long tradition of trading Black bodies for greenbacks. But lemme tell you how Black folks don't play with that *witchcraft* stuff—until they do.

Now known as Paula White-*Cain* after marriage number two, *Ms. Thing* enjoyed the trappings of being a spiritual advisor to the president. You couldn't turn on the TV or scroll through the news without seeing her and that bottle blonde hair takin' over the headlines and cable news clips for a solid four years. During the Wednesday night prayer service following the undeclared 2020 election, White-Cain called on "angelic reinforcement" from the continents of Africa and South America to secure Trump's reelection. She's up there on livestream hollerin', "I hear a sound of victory; the Lord says it is done!" Claimin' that angels were already dispatched from Africa and South America to save the day.

Mind you, this is the same Africa and South America that Cheeto Satan called "shithole countries," but she got the nerve, the unmitigated *caucasity*, to demand their labor in his favor. Black folks don't go for *none of that* when playing with things of the spirit. Still, we collectively knew that Paula was playing with some shit she underestimated. We all instinctively knew she was gon' mess around and get more than she bargained for. Because we don't believe in that *mess* until we do. We may debate the *nature* of witchcraft, but an unmistakable knowing within us doesn't deny its power.

> For what can be known about God is evident to them, because God made it evident to them. Ever since the creation of the world, his invisible attributes of eternal power and divinity have been able to be understood and perceived in what he has made.
>
> —Romans 1:19-20 NABRE

This may be difficult to process, but Christians do not have *exclusive* access to the knowledge of God. Like all other religions, Christianity is also concerned with the manifestation of the deity.

No religious faith, including traditional African faiths, could persist if God had not revealed Herself through creation. Through natural theological frameworks, even the "heathen" can sense the power and deity of God through creation. The doctrine of God in natural revelation sees God as the creator whose imprint on creation is indelible and serves as an omnipresent ruler of the created.

Within Ifa, there are sixteen guiding truths. The first of these truths is that there is one singular, supreme God called *Oludumare*—translating to almighty or supreme God in English. This follows a broad theme of religions among West African ethnic groups like Nyame of the Akan people of Ghana and Mawu by the Ewe in Benin. Honorifics in African religions indicate a reverence for God as creator and ruler. In Akan practices, God is called *Amowia* (giver of sunshine) and *Amosu* (giver of rain), expressing an understanding of God's providential care. An Akan proverb declares, "No one teaches a child to know God. God is self-evident." It reflects a faith that believes God is all around us, felt in the world around us, and yet still distinct from it.

Within these "heathen" practices, we also witness an understanding of God's judgment. Two common Akan sayings illustrate this concept: *ne tiboa bu ne fo* (their conscience has condemned them) and *Onyame mmpe bone* (God hates evil); the latter is echoed in the sentiments of the Black proverb, "God don't like ugly." There is another Akan phrase, *Nyame ntua woka* (God doesn't sleep), similar to the Black proverb of "He never sleeps nor slumbers" based on Psalm 121:4. These proverbs were not created in vacuums, and their present similarities despite centuries of distance are not merely *happenstance*.

The *heathen* experience of God through trees, animals, or even persons, dreams, and oracles closely resembles Old Testament experiences of God—and my own. I grew up cutting off televisions and lights during a storm before opening windows because *God was speaking* through the winds and rain. I learned to trust the reactions of babies and domesticated animals when someone entered a space because of their uncanny spiritual discernment. If a loved one tells me they've dreamed of fish, I'm quick to remind them that I have an IUD, but I have no doubt that the newly pregnant person will reveal themselves soon. I have always taken the revelation of God seriously, no matter how it comes. These experiences affirm what Romans 1:19 declares: God is revealed in diverse ways and forms, *and* there are revelations of a deity other than Jesus. For working-class Black folks in early twentieth century New Orleans, the revelation of God was found in the Spiritual Churches.

New Orleans, Louisiana, is easily in my top three favorite cities in America. My soul gets happy from the moment I set foot on the grounds of Louis Armstrong Airport. Everything I hold dear about this city finds its form in Blackness. The culinary delights of Ms. Linda, the YaKaMein Lady, hearing the linguistic delight of accented tongues thick with Southern drawls and the rhythmic influences of Creole, the musicality in how words are shaped as if each sentence is a carefully crafted composition. The cultivated joy, resilience, and communal connection are pitched in every note of jazz, bounce, and zydeco carried in the wind from car windows and breezeways. As I navigate the streets, I am reminded of the boundless influence of Black culture, the force that shapes every facet of this captivating city.

My visits are never without *visitations*, as the spirits of New Orleans are always present. It feels like the air is infused with the echoes of ancestors, their whispers of wisdom and strength resonating through time. It is rich with indigenous spiritual traditions of voodoo and hoodoo coexisting alongside Catholicism, creating a unique spiritual landscape that reflects the syncretic nature of Black faith traditions. Among these is the historical New Orleans Black Spiritual Churches, a loose confederation of Black churches that became sites of sanctuary, empowerment, and protest in the early twentieth century. These revered spaces cradled the hopes, dreams, and pains of those seeking solace within their walls. Their stories unfold, whispering prayers of sanctuary, nourishing the spirits of a community, and birthing the seeds of resistance.

The Spiritual Churches of New Orleans credit their start to Mother Leafy Anderson, a Black woman spiritualist and medium who relocated to the city from Chicago in 1920. In 1922 the National Spiritualist Association of Churches segregated and expelled its Black members, forming the Colored Spiritualist Association of Churches. Within a few years, Black Spiritualist churches were located in Chicago, Detroit, Philadelphia, and many other cities. The churches are linked to several denominations, including Protestantism, folk Catholicism, the Pentecostal movement, American Spiritualism, and vodun practices that survived the Black diaspora.[5] Their sanctuaries were known for their high aesthetic and their services for high emotionalism. These churches were distinguished by their organizational structure, beliefs, rituals, and particularly their practice of spiritual possession.

Trance-like states of dancing, spinning, violent fits, writhing, and falling out or "being slain in the spirit" mirrors the Pentecostal experience. Still, there is also the complex nuance of *multiple* spirit possessions. On the one hand, possession is attributed to *catching the Holy Ghost*—an attribute of the Trinity that Christians well understand. The second state of spirit possession is similar to *mounting* found among the *lwa* of Haitian Vodou and the *orisa* of Lucumí and Ifa. Spirit possession in the New Orleans churches involved *spirit guides* who, according to the belief system, include ancestors, biblical figures, Christian saints, or other venerated spirits. It is believed that the possessed person "works" with the spirit as an intercessor between themselves and God. As a member recalled: "These saints can overshadow you. They overpower you and have you talking like them. But we have the power to use and control these spirits, and they can use and control our bodies for their purposes."[6] For them, spirit possession offered an opportunity to labor in the spirit to shift their natural circumstances—not unlike the beliefs of present-day Black Protestantism.

I want to soothe any bristling discomfort at my mentioning of veneration, spirit guides, and the Holy Spirit in the same sentence. To reconcile this, it is worth considering that spirit guides are part of the sum of all good spirits that are in the Holy Spirit or, conversely, "That all such spirits are partial manifestations of the Holy Spirit."[4] It is worth reassociating these guides as a collective of ascended Christians who have lived according to God's laws and are now able to intercede for us in the spirit realm. Hebrews 12:1 tells a similar story: "*Therefore we also, since we are surrounded by so great a cloud of witnesses, let us lay aside every weight, and the sin which so easily ensnares us, and let us run with endurance the race that is set before us.*"

The word "therefore" implies that the writer is making conclusions based on previous statements in Hebrews 11. We're told everything about these witnesses of faith, summarily broken into four categories: those from before the flood—Abel, Enoch, and Noah; those before Moses: Abraham, Isaac, Sarah, Jacob, and Joseph; then the mosaic period of Moses himself; and finally, the post-mosaic period of the succeeding generations, including Rahab, who is named among others. At this point, the common thread between all of these people is they have all passed from the earthly plane. Yet, the writer saw fit to venerate, or regard with great respect, their lives and testimonies of God's acts in and through their lives.

The author reveres them so profoundly that they describe them as the great cloud of witnesses that inspire and influence the living to continue our faith race. Ancestral veneration does not contradict Christian theology, particularly the resurrection of Christ as the redeemer. To honor your ancestors means that you honor the example of their lives as a source of inspiration in developing our faith. The prayers, petitions, hopes, dreams, and invocations of our bloodline that have gone before us still carry, cover, and protect us. We know what God can do because we've seen Her perform in our lives and those before us—our *great cloud of witnesses.*

Christianity defines itself as a special revelation, suggesting that without the Christ narrative, it is impossible to know or experience the presence of God. Yet, generations of American enslavers, colonists, and missionaries held a revelation of God that reduced the Black diaspora to dehumanized subjugation. The same spirituality you've been convinced to fear is born of an unspoken oath among the collective: to dismantle the powers held by Christian slaves over their lives and bodies. The conjure work we've sermonized as demonic was evident in its power to alter outcomes. What we reject as witchcraft struck fear in the heart of the ruling class. For the enslaved African, as W. E. B. Du Bois points out, enslaved conjurers were the "healer[s] of the sick, the interpreter[s] of the unknown, the comforter[s] of the sorrow, the supernatural avenger[s] of wrong, and the one[s] who rudely but picturesquely expressed the longing, disappointment, and resentment of a stolen and oppressed people."[7] Any person or practice capable of liberating the oppressed will not be celebrated by those who benefit from oppression. It is no surprise that enslavers and their enablers demonized the retained practices of African spirituality and worship.

Christianity, as it arrived on American plantations, is "a contradictory, oppressive religion designed to impress upon the enslaved

African that their bondage had been preordained."[8] Its doctrine did not offer liberation, especially where decisions of when, where, and how enslaved Africans could worship were made *for* them. This faith has cast a long shadow of apprehension over Black lives. We find ourselves tangled in a web of self-doubt, wrestling with the distortions inflicted upon us by these beliefs.

Conversely, the birth of *hoodoo* provided familiar tenants of spiritual worship, including spirit possession, sacrifice, ritual water immersion, and divination. Without the transformation of the Black churches on Southern plantations by African spiritual connectedness, there would be no Black Church today. Without the creation of the "invisible institutions" that sought spaces far from the watchful eye of their enslavers, Black folks would be without an authentic revelation of God that reflects their *whole* image.

Our cultural values have been created for us by religious dogma indissolubly grounded in anti-Blackness. Consequently, our inherent mistrust in the legitimacy of our wisdom breeds a deep-seated fear. We perceive the very essence of our intuition as a treacherous force. Amid unfolding realities, we are confronted with a truth we can no longer ignore. The urgency of our circumstances demands that we shed the shackles of fear that have hindered our progress for far too long. As the world trembles under the weight of its contradictions, we can ill afford to remain paralyzed, cowering in the face of our shadow.

PREACHING FROM THE PEWS

I Did Everything Right

I did everything right.

I covered my head
My hands
My body
My desires
And my soul

I hid *me*.

Never spoke too loud
Unless agreeing with the oppressor.
Never too visible
Except for my femininity.
Never too independent
Except for when beauty in value and capital was not
enough.

I got my own house
Own car
Own means
And can take care of myself
I earned the worthiness of proximity
I gave myself fully and only to my legal owner
I cooked
I cleaned
I birthed
I enhanced

And when I was abused,
I evaluated how it was my fault and figured out how we could heal together

I loved
I shrunk
I taught others how to perpetuate, victimize, and survive the misogynoir too
I was the best mother
Best teacher
Best partner
Best help

I suffered, properly!
I know that I have never belonged to me
And made my wretched body a living sacrifice

I DID EVERYTHING RIGHT!

And "right" still wasn't salvation enough for what was left of me either.

—Valerie B

• 9 •

Between Juanita's Sheets

YOU CAN DO ALL things through Christ *except* wear Whore Red on Easter Sunday.

Valerie, my bestie, and I have an established routine of dressing one another before any important occasion. In the hours before any date, meeting, event, or church service, we catalog our wardrobes and finalize the details from head to toe during one of our multi-hour daily video calls. Val is, by all definitions, *fine as frog's hair* with deeply hued skin, an infectious smile, and the body of a dancer who has never lost her step. As shapely as she is agile, her petite frame presents few trouble spots—except those that caused her the pain of objectification. Styling her is always a delicate endeavor of balancing the push to stand out with deep awareness of the trauma of being *too* visible. Her body has been both celebrated and shamed. It has been as gently held as it has been deeply violated and required to hold more grief than it deserves. During our lives together, I've won a few negotiations with her aesthetic choices, but some conditions do not change, and the rules that govern her church wardrobe are among them. We are two of a kind in that way.

Her Baptist rearing in the Deep South of Galveston, Texas, ensures she minds her hemlines and doesn't step into a sanctuary without Lycra to stabilize her ample *assets*. She knows the rules of engagement—both stated and implied—within church culture for how women should present themselves in decency and in order. Picking an outfit is usually formulaic, settling on something modest and appropriate for the needs of service as a ministry leader or participant. But Easter is not just *any* Sunday service. Easter Sunday is the *Met Gala* of Sundays in the Black Church. In celebration of the risen savior, we assemble our finest apparel, which usually requires purchasing an entirely new piece of clothing, and step *out*! Easter, along with Christmas and Mother's Day, is the most well-attended worship service of the year, with everybody and *they mama* making sure they are in the house of the Lord. But on this night before Super Bowl Sunday for Jesus, our wardrobe planning hit a crisis. Deciding to paint her nails, she went rummaging to find a suitable nail polish, only to make a horrifying discovery.

"Sissy," she exclaimed in a panic, "I only have this sinner's red polish," she finished.

Without missing a beat, I retorted, "You mean *whore* red? Oh no."

We both sighed in lament, knowing this meant an emergency trip to the beauty supply store to find an appropriate replacement. The line fell silent as we both processed what this moment reflected about our conditioning and *contradictions*.

I'd be lying if I told you I didn't feel both conviction and a crisis of self when the words *whore red* left my lips. How could I, someone deep in the work of liberatory womanist praxis, immediately default to misogynoir-laden governance of women's bodies? I don't consciously associate red with sex work or promiscuity, but I wasn't allowed to wear red nail polish as a child because of it. At some point at the Black People National Convention, it was decided that red polish was off-limits, designated only for grown women equipped to handle what it advertised and invited. Yet here we were, deep in our womanhood, both innately knowing that somehow this red lacquer, *on Easter Sunday no less*, was dishonorable in the house of God.

The identity politics that structure the Black Church are richly complex, particularly for the Black women who comprise most of its population. The governance of feminine gender expression in this space is reinforced by the antagonism of *other* identities. You see, a *church girl* can't risk being too masculine or feminine in her appearance without triggering a rebuke. Unless it's an Apostolic church, a woman can wear pants to service, but if worn too frequently, *queerphobia* will beg the questioning of her sexuality. It is a culture that sees pants as a casual indulgence for women while remaining inherently masculine, at least as far as sanctuary dress codes are concerned. So a woman who appears to exclusively wear pants will launch whispers of wonder and not-so-subtle attempts by other women to feminize her, ensuring that she is not falling victim to the "spirit" of lesbianism. Still, not all *feminine* garments are created equal. The structure, length, height, and color of everything from camisoles to open-toed shoes make the difference between being seen as a virtuous Ruth or a shameless Rahab—even though both women engage in survival sex work, technically speaking, but that's a discussion for another time.

Gender performance is also dictated by *whorephobia*—the fear or shaming of sexually liberated individuals, specifically, sex workers. In our sanctuaries, this includes the fear of being *perceived* as overly sexual. Church girls are indoctrinated to be terrified of our bodies as sites of inevitable sin unless we are "clothed [in] strength and dignity," the embodiment of Proverbs 31 womanhood. When whorephobia meets the historical context of Black women as objects of lecherous, dangerous hypersexualization, we self-police our dress to protect our bodies *and* save our souls. It is why, despite knowing her body *is* her body, my bestie rejects any clothing that highlights her hip-to-waist ratio a little *too* well on Sundays and wouldn't dare to touch that red polish on Easter. For Black women, our churches are often the apex of our oppression at the intersection of sexism and anti-Blackness, where we do not know if the shame we receive about our bodies is merely because we are women or specifically because we are culturally Black women.

In the way that the elasticity of whiteness requires the static state of Blackness to sustain its power, identity politics of the Black Church requires misogynoir—a term coined by Black feminist writer Moya Bailey to describe the unique experience of misogyny for Black women where race and gender both play a role. I have often contended that the pulpit is the last bastion of power for the Black patriarchy. It is a refuge where Black men derive power often inaccessible to them within white supremacist power structures. In the institutional structure of our churches, for Black men to be powerful, Black women must be subjugated. This brand of misogynoir is fueled through sacrificial devotion as modeled by Proverbs 31, visible invisibility as demanded by Paul's silencing of women in 1 Timothy 2:11-12, and respectability politics that dictate both beauty and style for *respectable* women. Here, masculinity requires queer- and transphobic ideas of gender to make arbitrary inclusions and exclusions of people who get to access its power.

It also requires clobbering of biblical texts to define these gender normatives as the inerrant word of God to violently enforce its dominion. Brandi Miller writes that in many churches, "Women are easily interpreted out of relevance in the scripture and stripped of their power to liberate other women in church spaces, to lead and to be heard. The assumed and theologized inferiority of women (and, to a much greater extreme, trans women) reduces women to objects for men's use in a culture that insists on chasteness, humility, and purity. Women become submissive sidekicks or 'servants' who are granted participation in the church at the whim of male leaderships but rarely, if ever, power."[1]

And you can bet your bottom dollar that not all the guardians of Black patriarchy are Black *men*.

I was eight years old in the summer of '96 when T. D. Jakes took over our city with his inaugural gathering, Woman, Thou Art Loosed!, at the Georgia World Congress Center. Atlanta is a beautiful anomaly where, in 1996, it was home to *loose* women at Freaknik in the spring and *loosed* women in the summer, all while a little something called the 1996 Summer Olympics took place. Thousands of women flocked downtown for one purpose: to be "loosed" from the "shackles of abandonment, low self-esteem, addiction, and more to become victorious, secure women."[2] Following the typical conference format, its days were filled with varying breakout sessions, plenary discussions, and vendor markets, while its nights hosted full worship services with marquees of star-studded guest preachers. In its third year in 1999, the profile of the conference and one of its preachers would be catapulted into the national spotlight.

On a warm July night, Juanita Bynum, a charismatic prophetic evangelist, would begin her ascent to fame with her seminal message, "No More Sheets." The sermon excavates her personal narrative of struggling with her sexuality and perpetual singleness. The *sheets*, a demonstrative sermon prop, represented the emptiness of her sexual experiences with men and the subsequent bondage of the emotional brokenness left in their wake. Both the sermon and Juanita herself are the perfect encapsulation of the identity politics of Black churched women. We look for relief at the same altar where we are often lifted as a living sacrifice to maintain Black patriarchal power structures unique to our churches. This is no more evident than in the assembly of thousands of women at conferences designed to *fix* them. We spend hours in workshops, panel discussions, and talking circles that teach us how to serve the needs of others without learning how to create a fully realized self.

At the time of the sermon, Juanita is a forty-year-old divorced woman dealing with the grief of having "done everything right"—that is, as a woman raised in the dogma of the Church of God in Christ, having remained abstinent until marriage—and still ending up with the trauma of a bad mate. She narrates her life with the uncomfortable relatability of both Black woman resilience *and* resignation to suffering as a requirement for redemption. At one point in the sermon, she testifies of her lived experience:

> I've been married. I've had three miscarriages. I couldn't hold a child. I was told that I would never be nothing. I had a nervous breakdown behind my marriage; I was in an institution. The doctors said I would never be right. I almost died from anorexia. I was six months from being dead.[3]

She recalls a moment of despair where she tells God, "I can't take no more" and, in suffering Christian resolve, she claims, "The Lord said it's the process"[3] required for deliverance and restoration. This is an executive-level summary of the lived experience of Black women in relationship to their churches and faith. Our faithful devotion helps us make sense of our suffering, and our deliverance is predicated on our internal adjustments rather than dismantling systemic structures. *Lather, rinse, repeat.*

The rarity of the carte blanche authority and power loaned to Juanita Bynum (JB) that night cannot be understated. She comes from a denomination that denies women the call and ordination to preach or pastor churches. Even in more liberal church spaces where women are affirmed in ministry, we are still subject to gender performance. A woman must be high femme to work the pew, but she must also neutralize that femininity in the pulpit to eliminate any perception of threat. In the legacy of many before her, JB's visage that evening balances just enough feminine expression and repression to avoid alarm. Her hair reads as masculine in its shortly cropped style but is softened by skin-like makeup and delicate pearl earrings. Her two-piece suit is *pussy pink* but shows neither skin nor silhouette. The neckline is essentially up to her chin, and the matching skirt nearly sweeps the floor. The ensemble is formless and void, hiding any potential seduction from her *grown woman* body. JB solemnly observes in her opening lines of speech that "every time you mount a platform, there is a responsibility. And that responsibility is to make sure there is NO FLESH!"[3] Though this statement is not exclusively addressing her appearance in context, the multiple meanings are easily understood. The moment is a masterclass in charismatic ministry. Make no mistake: Juanita is as brilliant as she is controversial. She is culturally astute in all the ways necessary to navigate the treacherous pathways of Black *preachin'* women. It also makes her both a target and master guardian of church patriarchy.

On this night, Juanita takes her place on the platform and begins her exhortation saying, "The will of the Lord is in this place today. His will is here; His divine purpose is here." No central scriptures will anchor her message; instead, *No More Sheets* will be preached from the sacred text of JB's lived testimony and, as she describes, direct prophetic messages from God to birth "deliverance" within the audience. And for the next ninety minutes, she'll assail the flesh of 52,000 mostly Black women attendees as an unholy site needing excruciating sacrifice.

Sacrificial Devotion

Black women navigate the axis of, at minimum, three oppressive forces at any given time: anti-Black racism, classism—regardless of actual class stratification given the assumption of their class status due to anti-Black racism—and sexism both as a cultural aspect and an inherent sociopolitical structure. No matter how randomized the configuration, unambiguously Black women rank last in global patriarchal structures. White women are affected by the sexism of white men but are also protected and privileged by their whiteness over non-white men. Black men are maimed, imprisoned, and killed by racism but certainly exert their male privilege over the women in their community. Asian men from China to India are certainly impacted by colonial racism. Still, they may not hesitate to engage in the privilege of their maleness to women in their communities or the privileges of white proximity in their anti-Blackness toward my community. Black women are frequently named as the least preferred of romantic prospects but still socialized to be the nurturing support and backbone to the men who also despise and reject them. With few places of solace, Black women turn to religion and spirituality as critical tools to understand and cope with an adversarial world. We turn to the church in hopes that it will offer tangible understanding of *how* to remedy our social condition. Enter the *Proverbs 31 Guide to Sacrificial Devotion*.

Proverbs is home to a passage in its thirty-first chapter that has been polarized as the model of a "good woman." For twenty-two verses, Proverbs 31 describes the characteristics of the idealized virtuous, domesticated wife who is both an extension of her husband

and of the patriarchal status quo. Like other passages for both racism and homophobia, Proverbs 31 has been used as a proof text for the continued subordination of women in their relationships with men. The Proverbs 31 woman isn't completely absent of autonomous power, per se, as we see her making a land purchase in verse sixteen and working trade posts in verse eighteen. Still, her nobility and virtuosity are not in her self-determination but in the way she labors to the benefit of her husband and children. Effectively, for Black women, becoming like the Proverbs 31 woman—an unquestionably good, noble woman who is the perfect helpmeet for her mate—is the cure for our social condition. Becoming a Proverbs 31 woman is to take on a role where the best of one's actions still enable the lives of men to depend on and primarily profit from her labor. It asks women to feel empowered by being praised by men for their utility while being satisfied with being of secondary (and sometimes, tertiary if including their utility as a caregiver to children) importance. This kind of power—one that is present but not necessarily legitimized—is aligned with how Dr. Gerda Lerner defines patriarchy in her work, *The Creation of Patriarchy*:

> [. . .] means the manifestation and institutionalization of male dominance over women and children in the family and the extension of male dominance over women in society in general. It implies that men hold power in all the important institutions of society and that women are deprived of access to such power. It does *not* imply that women are either totally powerless or totally deprived of rights, influence, and resources.[4]

At its core, *No More Sheets* is another sermon in the tradition of making the sacrificial devotion of Proverbs 31 womanhood—that is, occupying roles devoted to enabling the lives of others at the expense of our own desires—*prescriptive* to the unique social conditions of misogynoir. It is important to note that this biblical passage describes worthy womanhood in the context of describing a suitable partner for a husband. Throughout her diatribe, JB lectures Black women and blames them for their own singleness due to their lack of domesticity, poor financial management, and "used" bodies. She unwittingly depicts Black women as mules unworthy of softness. Especially where softness in rest and the extensive care of others is seen as lazy and unbecoming of a "good woman." This is why when JB exclaims in rebuke that,

> When a man look at you, he see a major responsibility. When a man choose you, you ought to be able to say, "This is what I got right here." And see, the reason why you can't make the right decision when some fool come to you talkin' 'bout some, "Are you my wife?" is because you ain't got nothing! And the first pair of lamps he buy you, you all excited. "He bought me some lamps. He bought me this couch! He bought me my bedroom set." BUY IT YO' SELF![3]

The women in attendance that night responded to her with unanimous agreement and unusual vigor. We learn very quickly in our *girlhood* that *real womanhood* as Black women is always marked by our ability to labor. So it is not beyond our realm of understanding that our singleness is a critique of our worthiness *and* work ethic.

> Black women's work, time, and energy are yoked to obligatory institutional service and sacrifice, routinely justified through language of devotion to the communal

> body. This rationalization is a socially dangerous iteration of a white sacramental mentality. In it, Black women are positioned as eucharistic elements consumed for the function and wellness of the institution.
>
> — Dr. Oluwatomisin Oredein, Assistant Professor (Texas Christian University)[5]

To create inequity, you must either convince someone that they're inferior or create rules that codify them as being less than you. Gender inequality in church is not the will of God by the so-called natural order. It is a deliberate outcome of patriarchal culture at large and is especially heinous for Black women within our churches. In a world where we're already despised, exploited, and asked to suffer in silence, Black women flock to our churches that should be a refuge but often end up as sites of continued harm. Church patriarchy ain't your run-of-the-mill patriarchal oppression.

Studies on the psychology and sociology of religion have consistently found that Black women score higher than Black men on conventional measures of organizational, nonorganizational, and subjective religiosity and spirituality.[6-8] In other words, across every phase of life, Black girls, women, and elder mothers more frequently attend, participate in, and exhibit more intense religious commitment than other groups, including Black men. Historically, Black women have used the fundamental principles of Christianity as the basis for offering radical challenges to oppressive and dehumanizing social conditions.[9-10] In this way, our own religiosity is weaponized against us. It posits our subordination as a God-ordained way of life to edify the kingdom and be a good Christian woman. So we end up with a church full of unquestioning women who commit themselves to patriarchy in Jesus's name. And now we're out here being objectified, devalued, abused, and traumatized but calling it the will of God.

Respectability Politics

In addition to, or maybe *because* of, sacrificial devotion, Black churched women often subject themselves to external definitions of what makes them visible as *good women*. To be perfect helpmeets as romantic partners and fully devoted mothers, we are taught that good women are of respectable character as representatives of their partners, children, and community. Respectability Politics refers to women's movements in the Black Baptist church at the turn of the twentieth century. To save themselves from the harm of racist, sexist tropes assigned to them, Black women began to mimic the norms and values of white middle-class society. Margot Dazey notes, "in seeking to prove their respectable status, they distinguished themselves from 'unrespectable' Black women, thereby validating entrenched categories of social worthiness."[11] Hip Hop womanist scholar EbonyJanice Moore says of respectability politics:

> Respectability politics are defined as a set of beliefs holding that conformity to prescribed mainstream standards of appearance and behavior will protect a person who is part of a marginalized group, especially a Black person, from prejudice and systemic injustices. The politics of respectability is a form of moralistic discourse used by certain people, usually elders, public and prominent figures, leaders, and scholars—who are members of those various marginalized groups, asserting that to look, act, behave, dress, and present a certain way is to ensure safety inside of an anti-Black capitalist society.[12]

No More Sheets is preached as a warning of the consequences of being an "unrespectable" woman, and, by proxy, with lessons of how to "fix" us. Because a respectable Black woman is chaste at best and sexually discreet at least, JB wastes no time attacking the flesh of Black women as sites of their greatest sin. In explaining the problem of unmarried sex, Bynum describes sex as the spirit of a man stepping into your body. She claims, "Men are projectors, and women are receptive. [During sex] men release and women, they get an impartation." Her logical conclusion is that every time you have sex with someone, you marry them regardless of legal marital status. So promiscuous women who have too much sex have entered too many marriages and are "too spiritually married" to be considered a single, respectable woman suitable for real marriage. She goes as far as naming sexualized flesh as *toxic* and requiring stringent purification. She warns women in attendance who've engaged in premarital sex that "there's a penalty to pay for everyone you've slept with. You can stop thinking 'bout getting married because that's gon' take a while." When speaking on her own transition into respectable womanhood, she takes pride in naming that it allows her to "walk with my head held high because I don't belong to anybody, and pieces of me are not all over America," suggesting that consenting, pleasurable sex can never leave a woman whole or worthy when done outside the restrictive moral code of respectability.

Respectability Politics also frame our social worthiness for the statuses we seek and how we hope to be socially categorized. Again, Juanita sermonizes singleness as a cultural failing of Black women by attempting to explain why Black men choose to partner interracially:

> We always talkin' 'bout, "all our brothers is always going out and getting all these white ladies. What's wrong? We

> ain't good enough?" No! We're too needy! We ain't got nothing! I'm supposed to be a helpmeet! When you get ready to marry, what are you bringing to the table besides eyeliner and lipstick? You don't have a savings account. All yo' credit cards are run up. And now you want a rescue. The devil is a liar! God is calling you to accountability today![3]

She not only directly cites white womanhood as the litmus of respectability, but she also saddles Black women with the responsibility of overcoming the structural inequity that *upholds* white womanhood. If desirability is enough to venerate white womanhood, it is precisely because beauty must be denied to Black women as social capital. Suppose white women are privileged to avoid the requirement of financial prudence as a marital prerequisite. In that case, it is because Black women must bring more to the proverbial partnership table than *eyeliner and lipstick*. Black women must bring the exploited fruit of their labor to be crowned as worthy women because whiteness is enough of a helpmeet on its own in the politics of respectability. Black womanhood is shaped in a deficit, where our social worthiness as good is earned only by our willingness to persistently self-sacrifice to enable and *rescue* the lives of others with no expectation of reciprocity.

Visible Invisibility

> Even though African women form a large percentage of the South African population, they are typified by, amongst other behaviors, invisibility and silence. In the churches, they form the larger part of the membership but they have had virtually no sisters to interpret the

> Bible for them. Their humanity has been defined for them and the Bible has also been interpreted for them.
>
> — Dr. MJ Madipoane,
> University of South Africa[13]

The only threat greater to Black churched women than lacking sisters to interpret the Bible is the presence of sisters who interpret it through the lens of *patriarchal oppression*.

Let's be abundantly clear: the only way Juanita Bynum could fast-track from invited attendee to headliner in two years is through her demonstrated willingness to uphold the subordination of women under patriarchy. A woman vying for the privileges of the power of the pulpit must know that, at every turn, her male colleagues have very little interest in conceding power to someone who can destroy the entire system. She will be carefully vetted by watchful eyes on the lookout for even the faintest hint of a woman with liberation on her mind. So, believe me when I say that for her to go from attendee to speaker *that* quickly, she volunteered as tribute to the gatekeeping of Black-preacher-alpha-male bullshit. And believe you me: most times, the women are more phallocentric than the ones with actual phalluses.

Juanita doesn't just show up this night as an agent of misogynoir; she embodies it with vigor in the perfect masculine intonation of Black preaching cadence. Her rebukes are shot through deep-throated vibrato coded with specific disdain for women. Her voice booms through that auditorium like thunder with every decree, casting and calling out everything that problematizes this indisputable Black, femme flesh. She convinces thousands of Black women—and herself—that their failure lies in this irredeemable femme flesh. Flesh that serves as nothing but cemeteries for the spirits of men long gone from our lives and hearts. She defends patriarchal protection against the inquiry of its accountability for its role in our failures. There is no similarly structured biblical proverb or *wisdom* offering for the makings of a virtuous husband. From the story of Eve being formed from the rib of Adam as a helpmeet to the woman whose children shall rise and call her blessed, the biblical narrative of women is often told from the perspective of an androcentric world. It is a world where women matter, but they never matter enough for *themselves*. It is a sacred text where women give birth to the savior and the gospel of salvation, but many more women are nothing more than unnamed plot devices as some man's daughter or another man's wife. I guess Brother James Brown was right: it's *a man's world*, but it is incomplete without women as props.

But now we find ourselves in a time where the *girls* of the women loosed from the '99s and 2000s of Juanita's sheets are sprouting deep roots into our loosening womanhood. And at this point, the math just ain't mathin', y'all.

> Don't mess with me! I'm on a mission for God! I'm not fallin' for no junk. I don't want your car! I don't want your house! I don't want no TV! I don't want no lamps! I got a house! I got a car! I got some lamps! I got a couch! Are you saved? Do you have integrity? Is your bills paid? I don't know about y'all, but I wanna be free. I WANNA BE FREE!
>
> —Juanita Bynum, No More Sheets[3]

Juanita's instructions to us were to redeem ourselves by remaining single. It was clear as day. In closing the sermon, she admonishes all who look on that when they "leave outta this conference, [God] don't want you going outta here wit' yo' mind on gettin' married. But He wants you to leave outta here wit' yo' mind on gettin' SINGLE!"[3] Aight, Auntie. Bet. *Vas-y*. Copy that.

We were told that we could and *should* do bad all by ourselves to be in both service to and deserving of the romantic partnership we valued. We believed that and decided we could also do better for ourselves than pursuing a life enabling men who cannot protect and provide for us. We were told to repair our lives to need men less and find contentment within ourselves more. It's funny when we are now chastised for becoming the *loosed* women we were groomed to be.

"We are raising our women to be men! Stop bragging about how much you don't need me and wonder why I shy away!" – Bishop T. D. Jakes, Father's Day 2022 Service at The Potter's House

Between tusslin' with these damn sheets and T. D. Jakes mouth-breathin' into the mic on *Father's Day* to call *Black women* masculine, I'm exhausted. What the hell am I fighting so hard for when churches still make room for and uphold this kind of bullshit on *every* Sunday? Y'all still asking women to shrink. Still preaching to us as the problem AND problem solvers. Still shackling misogynoir to virtuous womanhood and calling it God's word. I believed Juanita's witness when she said I could be FREE if I purged myself of all the toxic attachments to people, places, and things unworthy of taxing my womanhood. Choosing myself as worthy is the most virtuous thing I will ever do.

Exactly three years after the seminal moment *No More Sheets* pushed her into the national circuit, Bynum found and married the reward of her labor into virtuous womanhood. She and Bishop Thomas Weeks III married in July 2002, nine months before a ceremony televised on the Trinity Broadcasting Network that included an eighty-member wedding party and a ten-piece orchestra. By June 2007, the pair were separated as their troubles burst into media headlines on August 21 of that same year after Weeks was arrested for attacking his estranged wife in the parking lot of Atlanta's Renaissance Concourse Hotel. By the following June, their amicable divorce was finalized. She has not been publicly partnered since.

That's the complex thing about internalized misogynoir: one is both a participant and victim in their own oppression. Do you know why I *have* to hold space for Juanita despite her repeated betrayals of sisterhood?

I have to hold space for Juanita because she is still a woman who has been repeatedly harmed by men she loved. Husbands she vowed to honor with the strength and dignity of the *respectable woman* she was raised to be despite the odds. Men she trusted in ministry to hold up their end of the bargain for her betrayal who double-crossed her at the first moment of vulnerability. She is still a Black woman like me, deeply wounded by the promises of a purity culture not built to protect the outcomes of girls like us. The ones who do everything right and still have to mend the trauma of men who didn't value you enough not to harm you. She is still a Black woman whose body couldn't hold a baby where one was so desperately desired. She is a grieving mother, weeping tears over children she never got the chance to hold but still forever deeply loved. She is a woman with a broken contract with God for what she expected to receive in exchange for her self-sacrifice.

I also choose to have critical grace for Juanita because few others will. Unlike when I criticize Pastors—and I use that word *very* loosely here—Mike Todd, John Gray, or Bishop T. D. Jakes, very few people will say that Juanita's words are decontextualized and posted to make her look bad. TikTok-seconds-long clips of her sermonic ranting shared far and wide across social platforms are enough to draw permanent conclusions, public ridicule, and eventual dismissal. No one will call for grace whenever she speaks in her next viral clip. No one will ask me to understand the intention of her words. Nobody defends the women in our churches, including and perhaps *especially* other women. I've witnessed the willingness to sacrifice anyone to gain temporary proxy access to patriarchal power. It's a thrilling, intoxicating power that is tempting to even the most *liberated* of women.

Still, I wonder how many women who cried and tarried for their deliverance that night in 1999 are still wrestling alone in the emptiness between Juanita's sheets some twenty-five years later.

P.S.—Juanita, if you're reading this, I just wanna say, before you block me on everything, that I never go to church with my legs all greased up, looking like a deacon finna do me over in the corner, or let my sister wear whore red on Easter—all because of you. Thanks, Auntie!

· 10 ·

The Men All Pause

BY NOW, YOU'VE NOTICED that I intentionally refer to God in the masculine *and* the feminine. Mother God. She. Her. It disrupts our fixed notions of God as being exclusively male. When we trouble our theological narratives of gender, I believe we welcome equality and justice into our spiritual lives. This soft linguistic shift expands the multifaceted aspects of the Spirit. It is a solicitation for a more inclusive, holistic understanding of God. It affirms all gender identities as divine. More than that, I love to feminize God as a satisfied *middle finger salute* to the rampant misogyny so often committed in Jesus's name. The patriarchal structures that have historically marginalized and oppressed women are shaken in *Her* name.

Yet, a haunting question lingers: How can I reconcile my creation in the image of a masculine God with a concept of womanhood that condemns every aspect of my being as inferior to men? This inquiry has dominated every corner of my self-reflection in my search for a God like *me*.

Naturally, having been raised in the Black Church, an expansive gendered view of God was not part of the experience. In a pretty striking observation, I only recall an elusive presence of femininity within the descriptions of the divine. A *womanish* God often confined to the sporadic song lyrics crooned in loving memories of distinctly Black mamas who've gone on to glory. Or in the improvised embellishments of preachers in the crescendo of a closing sermonic whooping. In those precious moments, God is summoned as a "mother to the motherless," an ephemeral glimpse into the sacred feminine. Beyond these fleeting glimpses, the divine is invariably depicted as resolutely masculine. This realization begs questioning the dynamics of religious spaces, where women are relegated to roles as ushers, nurses, and choir members. At the same time, the pulpit remains predominantly the domain of men. This unquestioned arrangement pervades our collective consciousness, leaving little room for inquiry or resistance, even within myself. It is a curious, deeply ingrained and rarely challenged acceptance that calls for contemplation. A *selah*, if you will.

I never pondered the gender of God as a child, but I remained keenly aware of the constraints that loomed over me. By virtue of being a woman, I internalized a sense of inherent sinfulness—a burden I carried in solitude. Years of indoctrination told me that piety is what made me good. Many sermons about gender focused on becoming a wife, being a better wife, or guarding myself from being the object of lust by men. I only saw women get called out for the *big sin*—at least in the absence of queer masculine bodies to antagonize. I watched teenage girls get forced to publicly repent for their pregnancies while the men who caused them remained unaccounted for. I witnessed women get disfellowshipped for *sins* committed with men who maintained their positions in ministry. What I learned of my womanhood from the church stood in stark opposition to the character of God as I knew it.

There is no shortage of prescriptive sermons on the attributes of godly womanhood nor the accompanying rebukes of an ungodly one. Churches hyperfocus on who, how, and what women should be to be good wives, mothers, and people without giving men that same energy. I wonder, if boys aren't being onboarded into their expected gender performance in churches, what *are* they hearing about the role of *their* masculinity in lectures on *our* womanhood?

Allow me to borrow Stacy C. Boyd's question to answer *my* question: "How do race and religion play into the construction of what it means to be masculine in the USA?"[1] Religion has formed religious constructs of gender the world over. The Black Church constructs what it means to be Black, male, and Christian. It has defined the performance of masculinity and lends itself as a forum for negotiating its limits in pulpits. I wonder if men are as curious about what our churches have posited as God's masculinity says about their own. As Boyd suggests, I wonder if there is an anxiety in Black male negotiations with constructions of Blackness, maleness, and Christian embodiment. Where the role of women is explicitly framed in our sacred spaces, the place of men is strongly implied. In the absence of instruction, you imagine the lesson.

It's no secret that women are the lifeblood of the church. We are responsible for its past, present, and future stability as the lion's share of its membership. We bring our time, talent, money, and children, should we decide to mother. We have literally birthed every generation of church membership. We lift the institution as the North Star of our morality and sociocultural expectations of race, gender, and Christian embodiment. When little boys hear "Be the man of your house" and "Women, submit yourselves to your husbands," what does that tell them about power and who should have it? Little boys *see* all the people in the pulpit are men. They also *see* the ones guarding the doors (ushers), fixing food, and creating a welcoming space as women. What does that communicate about leadership and the role of protection within it?

I think we must answer how Christian ethics influence the construction of masculinity, especially Black masculinity. If we decide to view Mary's pregnancy as a result of non-consent by a deity, how does this influence the construction of masculinity? If every word of the Bible is infallible, how does the sexual assault of Bathsheba form our ideas of *godly* masculinity? How does Paul's dominant biblical discourse of silencing women influence it? What if these things succinctly demonstrate that it is a man's Christian *duty* to violate, dominate, and silence women? *Imagine* the tension of deciding if you'll embody God's masculine protector-provider aspect or His dispassionate authoritarianism and violence.

> "In a word, the anxiety can be forged out of a policing done by religion, race, and sexuality. Policing defines what is essential, authentic, and nondeviant."
>
> —Dwight N. Hopkins and Linda E. Thomas[1]

Studies of Black masculinity argue that Black men have been struggling with normative white masculinity, especially as whites attempted to link manhood to racial dominance.[1] I believe that *church patriarchy* is born out of this struggle. Religious patriarchal ideology socializes us to believe that men should have more power, dominance, and privilege than women and children, and that it is God's will.

Here, masculine power is meaningful by defying everything that is not feminine. Feminine power becomes meaningful through its docility and willing *submission* to masculinity. The fate of this is an exhausting pursuit of perfect gender performance for the reward of power. Judith Butler notes in *Gender Trouble* that "Men and women perform masculinity and femininity while the specific boundaries of those performances must be continually reinforced—the performance is not natural to bodies. Instead, the enforcement of these performances supports traditional systems of power and inequality deeply rooted in racist patriarchal Western culture."[2]

For years, the noise of political punditry and news media cycles has focused the collective Black imagination on the erasure of Black men and masculinity. We're losing them to the prison industrial complex where they're over-indexed as 38 percent of the US prison population. They're lost to conservative politics and racial transgressions of *selling out*. Queerphobia convinces us that trans and same-gender loving identities leech *masculine power* out of our communities. The anxiety of this erasure is in the pregnant silence between the *very loud* demands of Black womanhood in our religious dogma. Speaking to men about what is essential and authentic to manhood might reveal our uncertainty of what defines Black masculinity when we decenter white patriarchy.

The history and culture of masculinity has always been problematic. The rejection of gender as immutable by both feminist and queer identity politics has only amplified this trouble. The "crisis" of disappearing Black masculinity is that the demands of capitalism, including the social capital of stable romantic partnership, require Black men to respond in new and different ways. We live in the wake of ineffective models of *virtuous masculinity* in our churches. By viewing gendered power in religious terms, the *loss* of masculinity is either God's will to test one's faith or God's *wrath* as a consequence of sin. This rationale leads to an insistence on maintaining existing systems of social inequality. The intersection of race, gender, and religion has created a complex landscape where masculinity is both shaped and constrained by theological doctrines.

Out of its anxiety, Christian theology perpetuates notions of Black masculinity that align with white, patriarchal ideals. Strength, dominance, and control are emphasized, while vulnerability, tenderness, and emotional expression are discouraged. This narrow view of masculinity, particularly when theologized as holy, has limited the range of identities available to Black men who hope to satisfy the tension of their identity and Christian embodiment. The struggle for dignity in a religious tradition that has been complicit in our subjugation is an ongoing challenge for those seeking to reclaim their identities and assert their humanity. It requires treacherous navigation of the tension between cultural realities and religious expectations. As the demands of men to respond as men in whole new ways increase, many are left struggling to find a sense of self that integrates both aspects of their identity.

Perhaps the maintenance of supremacist thinking and power is what the church *has* best implied about the role of Black masculinity. Pulpit commands about moral Black Christian womanhood certainly reflect the patriarchal power struggle of Black and white men. Male dominance is a learned, not innate, feature of Black masculinity. bell hooks agrees, saying:

> Even those coming from communities where sex roles shaped the division of labor, where the status of men was different and most times higher than that of women, had to be taught to equate their higher status as men with the right to dominate women, they had to be taught patriarchal masculinity. They had to be taught that it was acceptable to use violence to establish patriarchal power. The gender politics of slavery and white-supremacist domination of free black men was the school where black men from different African tribes, with different languages and value systems, learned in the "new world," patriarchal masculinity.[3]

Our imagining of God as exclusively male must be troubled for its implication on how we perceive patriarchal masculinity. The fervent proclamation of women's worth while maintaining an ominous silence on men reflects inherited Christian theologies steeped in dehumanizing narratives that erode our agency. Our liberation is tantamount to our recognition of the feminine as an inherent and essential aspect of the divine.

Merely contemplating a God that transcends the confines of maleness opens doors to reimagining spirituality, ethics, and social relations. Virtues traditionally associated with femininity—nurturing, compassion, interconnectedness—shine forth as sacred and worthy. This shift in perception reconfigures our understanding of God and invites a broader reevaluation of gender roles. It compels us to confront gender equality, making an urgent task of dismantling the oppressive structures woven into the fabric of our religious and secular realms. Benevolent patriarchy will not save us; perhaps masculinity redefined beyond the deviant scope of supremacist ideals will.

• 11 •

Soft, Heavy & Black

Like many whose gender identities are forged in the fires of surviving the double jeopardy of Blackness and femininity, my mama didn't raise me to be an *easy* woman. I am a cisgender Black woman, and much of this is written from this perspective. I know the frustration of reading between the lines of other people's experiences to find *myself* included within them. My usage of collective pronouns like "us," "we," and "our" is done with the explicit inclusion of all Black marginalized genders. Our experiences have varied nuances, but witnessing yourself within my lived experience is not by happenstance.

My autonomy has deep, sprawling roots. My social matriculation through womanhood focused on a curriculum of hyper-independence. The objective was to build financial and emotional security in the absence of a man—a constant contradiction to the church's insistence that the zenith of my life could only be found through a submissive wife- and motherhood. The emphasis on independence, in my experience, was rooted not in misandry—a deeply ingrained contempt for men—but a reactionary course correction from witnessing the struggles of women before us who found themselves at the mercy of undesirable partners because their livelihoods depended upon it. Marriage to my daddy hadn't rescued my mama from economic disparity, and her subsequent divorce certainly didn't help matters. Her sixty-hour work weeks at the county job that barely covered our needs came at the expense of her presence and my abrupt exit from the sheltered harbor of ignorance to the realities of adult obligations. I was a latch-key kid learning the domestic skills of cooking, cleaning, and household management before I reached double digits. Mama's fierce independence was not anomalous to my friends' mothers or my mother's girlfriends, so my association with hard work and real womanhood became cemented as a universal experience of all women who looked like me.

My understanding of what defines Black womanhood is something I come by honestly. The formation of the *Cult of Domesticity* or *True Womanhood* in the antebellum period of the nineteenth century never intended to include room for Black women's pious, soft docility by its inherent nature. Its gender role ideology was designed to only outfit upper- and middle-class white womanhood and establish the bar to strive toward by poor white women. Barbara Welter, who coined the term *Cult of True Womanhood* in 1966, lays bare the reality:

> The attributes of True Womanhood, by which a woman judged herself and was judged by her husband, her neighbors and society could be divided into four cardinal virtues—piety, purity, submissiveness, and domesticity. Put them all together and they spelled mother, daughter, sister, wife—woman. Without them, no matter whether there was fame, achievement or wealth, all was ashes. With them, she was promised happiness and power.[1]

Where white women's education instilled these *cardinal virtues* of subordination that undergird heteronormative patriarchy, Black women weren't even factored as human beings, let alone seen as women capable of piety and purity. Even with our submissiveness already beaten into and *out* of us through enslavement and our masterful domesticity acquired in the same way, we were still left a day late and a dollar short for cult inclusion. *Their* violent sexual assault robbed *us* of *true womanhood's* purity. Our complicated Christianity that emphasized the *divine purpose* of our dehumanization through enslavement obscured our piety, while the innate fragility of being a woman was "the antithesis of most Black women's lives during slavery and for many years thereafter."[2] Black people's educational philosophy, then, had to set its sights on a gender-neutral goal of racial uplift that improved the socioeconomic outcomes of enslaved-to-emancipated people.

From the outset, Black women were tasked with prioritizing the fight for *racial* equity before pondering their own gender ontology. Even as the importance of gender is readily acknowledged by Black folks for Black folks, as is noted by the inclusion of gender identifiers in the titles of religious, civic, and academic organizations formed at this time, Black women's emerging self-awareness was first grounded in recognition of their oppression by their race rather than their gender. Every accomplishment, from education to employment, was done with the ethos of *racial uplift* in mind. Black women were an economic, sociopolitical necessity to their families *and* race. Black women primarily bore the burden of *lifting as we climb* through academic advancement. They were prominent fixtures of the migratory movements of educated Blacks to the South to help transition others from enslavement to freedom—without regard for gendered power or dynamics. As Black men's education rates began to shift, so did the attitudes for women's place by community members. The number of Black men who held degrees was ten times more than that of Black women by 1890.[2] She further notes that during and after the Reconstruction period, those educated Black women were trained almost exclusively to become elementary and secondary school teachers. Despite their small numbers, educated Black men had more encouragement and access to institutions of higher education as well as greater employment opportunities than Black women. With the passage of the Fourteenth Amendment establishing gendered rights *and* sociopolitical validation of Black manhood, the acquisition of voting rights and federal, state, and local political positions brought with it Black men's adaptation of white society's attitudes toward womanhood.

Once they got on, they tried to leave our asses for a feeble imitation of white patriarchal supremacy, complete with gaslighting Black women's observed experiences when confronted by them. It should come as no surprise then that Black women today, the fruit of our foremothers' gardens, find themselves in the paradox of rejecting intraracial patriarchal oppression while still feeling deeply obligated to the safety and protection of our sons, fathers, brothers, lovers, and kin—and why we measure our utility through our own silent long-suffering. The shifted weight of communal uplift from one of an egalitarian endeavor to a paternalistic burden heaved upon our shoulders has never been properly redistributed. In trying to save ourselves from post-slavery demise, we measured the success of our *racial uplift* by how well we could model *white society* whose manic love for corrupted power, money, and hegemony was often out of integrity with our lived realities. And, like everything molded by white supremacy, we are collectively cracking beneath its unbearable weight.

• • •

When I reached the rites of passage into womanhood, understanding the blessing of a Black girl child who had her own was the hallmark of being a real woman. My Black consciousness emerged in the era where the Million Man March meets *Waiting to Exhale*—both events happening mere months apart the year I turned seven. Of course, I wasn't allowed to watch the film until I was much older, but that didn't stop me from singing "Not Gon' Cry" with indignation like John had left *me* for a white woman too.

While doing my best to be seen and not heard during long Saturday mornings at the beauty shop, I bore witness to the conversations between women where one of the film's protagonists, Bernadine "Bernie" Harris, became both an affirmation of knowing *and* a cautionary tale of how you can't trust these men. Bernie's abandonment by her husband despite her faithful devotion and self-sacrifice was held up as a *Parable of the Fool*, the consequence of giving away your power as a woman. And on the following Sunday mornings, I sat in the sanctuary pews and heard that women should submit themselves to these same men as the head of their households and marriages to please God.

My thirteenth birthday brought with it my freshman year of high school, a palpable interest in dating, and Beyoncé singing my ideas of womanhood with her words in "Independent Women Pt. 2." *Strong* women provided for themselves by their own means. *Free* women could choose romantic partnerships but by no means defined their worth by their relationship status. I dreamed of being one of the *money-making women* Bey crooned about who could *do what I want, live how I wanna live*.

After my first serious crush rejected me—the girl he spent hours talking on the phone with and getting to know—in favor of the light-complected girl who ignored his existence, I quickly understood that some girls *choose* independence. For others it is chosen *for* them. I ain't never been a small thing; by the time I reached my sophomore year, I was already shopping exclusively in the only three stores available to me with ample floral and animal print options that I can only assume designers believed would hide the horrors of my portly body. In the power of desirability, I lacked erotic and beauty capital needed to succeed. I was pretty *for a big girl* and dark-skinned—an acceptable brown but not *too* dark. Having *good hair*—long when straight and curly when natural—added to my pretty points, but not enough to place top five on any boy's list. Where I lacked in physical desirability capital, my gregarious wit gave me a leg up in the social hierarchy. Where boys didn't see me as a *honey* and girls didn't see me as competition, they saw me as the *fat funny homie* who ridiculed myself before letting someone else cut me to the quick. With my unrequited school crushes, I turned to the church in search of a godly boyfriend who, I assumed, would see the whole me and not just the potential pleasure of my *holes*. I had more success with church boys and their willingness to date me, but trust me when I say they put the HOE in holiness. Deeply rooted in purity culture, my uncompromised virginity became my bargaining chip and pedestal. I was praised by the church community for saving myself and following God's command, but truthfully it's easy to live holy when nobody wants you to *sin a lil' bit with 'em* to begin with.

I've been self-aware of my perceived attractiveness and rank in social strata for as long as I've desired to date. I've had two serious long-term relationships as an adult with a few sneaky links to scratch the itch, but I have never felt true safety with any of my romantic partners. I have always thought that I was too much, physically and emotionally, and not enough at the same damn time.

As a fat Black woman, my body is often defeminized, given my five-foot-nine height and weight. My fat body is both invisible and hyper-visible, a target for the projections of others and erased when my story refuses to fit the desired narrative of self-hatred or to exist as an apology. Those of us whose bodies are neither frail nor diminutive in stature are often assumed to possess strength that can withstand abuse and be undeserving of tenderness. Our bodies become sites of intimidation, and we're told that physical violence against us could be a rational response due to our size. Sex with us is too often used as a training ground to perfect a skill set intended to be the reward for someone whose *fineness* is worthy of exquisite pleasure. Our partners are praised for looking *past* our bodies and seeing our *true* beauty despite the egregious sin of our adipose tissue.

In a world where I have to pray that they like fat girls at *best* or, at least, that they don't act a fucking fool because someone might *think* they could be attracted to a fat girl, is it any wonder why I am not a soft woman? Every romantic decision I've made in my life has been for self-preservation. My feminist idealism of an equitable partnership—always going fifty-fifty in relationships—was as much a survival mechanism as it was an ethos. With my well-worn ideas of *real womanhood* grounded in labor, I convinced myself that showing up as both breadwinner and emotional laborer in my relationships was simply what should be done. Despite having neither my emotional, sexual, or financial needs met, I believed myself to be equally yoked *and* safe from the dependency on someone else's provision. I know better now.

Still, like many of my peers, I've been so consumed with course correction for every personal, romantic failure I've committed and for what we've collectively demonized women from previous generations that it feels like we've scorched earth that has yet to bear fruit. Mama raised me with a hermeneutic of suspicion witnessing the all too familiar experiences of women's perilous existences when subject to the emotional whims of paternalism. Often the prescriptive advice of elders is rooted in a deep love and fear of knowing this world will only make room for us when we adhere to certain codes—and even then, it's a maybe. Be clear: I am under no illusion that every single Black foremother had or *has* our best interest at heart. I'm painfully aware of the heightened dysfunction between jealous mothers and their embittered daughters. For every Black woman who speaks truth to power, some trade on their diversity factors to shuck, jive, and bask in the waning light of white gaze. I am speaking instead of the cloud of great witnessing Black women who see our lived experience at the intersections of misogynoir, anti-Blackness, and other marginalization as necessary to dismantle, not Black women who take every opportunity to instead blame us for our oppression.

We've accurately assessed that many of our predecessors "settled" in relationships/marriages that they could not easily dissolve due to financial dependence. Our response has been a course correction of hyper-independence. For every foremother trapped by the perils of lacking formal education, we correct it by devoting years to academia and careers before hitting forty-plus and recognizing we desire intimate companionship. We saw women's financial and emotional struggles before us and decided the corrective was hypergamy and divestment from our ethnic community as a suitable eligibility pool. We've recognized how our sexuality has been vilified, but we've not quite figured out that being sexually provocative isn't always the same as being sexually liberated. At this point, I don't know if you can tell a Black woman in my peer group that she's contributed to her own life's dissatisfaction—not solely responsible for, but certainly played a role—lest you be met with accusations of anti-Blackness, specifically misogynoir. What we've learned not to do to obtain unprecedented freedom is because our foremothers had a greater sense of accountability in ways and situations that we often do not. We know at our core that the zenith of our womanhood isn't our ability to be partnered. The point is the liberation and the body of work we leave to women behind us as they pick up the fight for intersectional equity.

And what the podcast bros and pick-me divine feminine girls see as *masculine energy* has merely been our means of surviving a world that leaves girls like me unprotected. While I was taught to survive without a man *just in case*, I was also socialized to support men as a helpmeet. Whether as a female friend, relative, or partner, I've always been asked to see myself in the support role of men. As a Southern Black womanist, all facets of my socialization are rooted in facilitating the support of Black men, especially their need to be needed. I have a praxis that sees how white supremacy, patriarchy, and capitalism have exploited and harmed men. I've had to uproot internalized misogynistic beliefs about Black women who do not contribute labor to shared finances and domestic duties *because* I thought it was unfair to put the onus of survival and provision solely on the backs of Black men, who too are only making pennies on the white man's dollar. To my detriment, I've made room as the softness and landing spot for men I dated beneath my life station, thinking that all he needed was to be uplifted to his best and highest self. My reward for my martyrdom has been, in the short term, heartbreak and peculiar singleness in its much longer realm. I've been desexualized and mammified or codified as a healer, a stop on the way to someone else who benefits from my labor. The softness I'm accused of not having is the same softness that strips me of being seen as sensual or sexual. Even at the height of my corporate success, it never negated my socialization to make room to both affirm and validate my last partner. "I don't need you" has never been part of my community, kinship, or relationship framework. Still, making room to "need" men is not enough when soft, powerhouse women are between the rock of desirability politics and the hard place of being undesired.

This world has all too often told me that I am unworthy of the tenderness I crave, but as always, I've chosen to fight back. I deserve ease, grace, and tenderness because it is what I desire, and my desires don't have to be earned and rewarded by the size of my body or the hue of my skin.

In the continuous singleness in the years after the breakup that nearly broke me, I was willing to do whatever it took to be a more palatable partner to the kind I wanted. Softness said to shrink the hardened parts of me. The ambition sired by my struggle, the aggression birthed from a never-ending stream of challenges, my strength forged by the fear of certain death if I succumbed to my weakness.

As a Black woman, I've never been afforded the resources to *have it all*. I must be the leader at work, leaping twice as high and working thrice as hard. I must come home and then switch to the submissive role to not emasculate my partner. The pride and pain of Black womanhood is our incomparable resilience. It fuels the flames of both our survival and, ultimately, our demise. So, I can't afford to be broken or *soft* in ways that insist on giving my vulnerability to chance and the charitable capriciousness of power structures.

The idea of *softness* and *soft life* became a beacon in the unending dark night of my own *Strong Black Womanhood*. I have willingly taken on more than I could or should handle: my pain, the pain of partners I chose to love, and the painful plight of my community. Black women are the mothers of those murdered by state-sanctioned violence as well as its overlooked victims; we are the forgotten daughters; we are the champions on the frontline confronting the never-ending injustices of our communities. We pull it together. We hold it together. We are so good at being a savior to everyone else that we forsake ourselves. The Cape of Black Womanhood is one we often suit up with pride. Our survival depends on our ability to lay aside our humanity to assume immortality for those around us. Each role we play in life is subject to depths of criticism unique only to us. Patriarchy requires our perfection as mothers, lest we be held responsible for the increasing rates of single-parent homes. Capitalism requires that we navigate work environments that often despise and ridicule us, forcing us to code-switch our tongues and relax our strands for the relaxation of others. Even in our dogged tiredness, we dare not ask for or hire help to free ourselves up. Yet, even when breathing feels like a herculean effort, we proudly display our capes as our strength.

They told me softness demands my roar become a docile whisper. I believed softness meant my hair, even in braids, needed to be long. That my femininity—destabilized by the size of my body, the crookedness of my smile, the deep hues of my skin—could only be redeemed by the looseness of my natural curl pattern that unfurled to waist length when stretched. I believed them when they told me that only designer leather goods draped over my shoulder could signal my belonging. I built up a softness that smelled of saccharinely sweet floral vanilla fragrances, convinced my true love of woodsy musks like cedar and sandalwood might betray my appearance of femininity. It was a softness that blotted away any reflection of my most authentic self. I'm a five-foot, nine-inch Black woman with a body that is the pinnacle of softness. This adipose tissue lives and breathes softness—a respite where weary heads lie. I am already soft enough. What was I trying to fix?

I wanted softness to remediate my undesirable parts—the *angry* Black woman, the *independent* Black woman, every inch of myself that made me unfit for consumption by the *good ones*. The gift of being all things to all things is the ability to forget ourselves in favor of martyrdom. We nurture partners/spouses who are often neither our equal nor our savior at the expense of ourselves. The Christ complex within us convinces us that we can transform people into wholeness by offering our love wholesale. We eagerly pay the tariffs of our emotional and, in some cases, physical well-being in a gamble for the love and affection of emotionally unavailable people. If we didn't, we'd otherwise be forced to pay the high price of singleness. After all, the years of grooming in our relationship ethics teach us that singleness is an acquiescence of our brokenness. Being broken is an exposure of our flaws. Brokenness reminds us of our emptiness, sadness, and open wounds. My need to feel safe is in constant opposition to my need to save myself from real and imagined threats. Self-preservation pushes me to stay one step ahead, prepared to pick up the pieces for *when*, not *if* someone leaves me. I cannot give space to my own fractures because the cost of betraying myself as weak in any regard is one I've not been willing to pay again.

Even with my best efforts, my pursuit of softness only hardened to deepened resentment. No matter what I did, wore, or spoke, that softness would never be accessible. Softness must be more than what we wear, where we fly or dine, and how we speak to the fragility of unequipped partners to honor our totality. I realized I was not unhappy with myself; I was only unhappy to live in a world where being all of me is never enough. Softness, or femininity, then represented what I believed would give me access to a world where I was valued and cared for and not have my worth measured by how much of my labor could be extracted at the lowest possible cost. I wanted softness that freed me from the weight of my cape. I wanted softness that felt safe enough to cede control of my care and safety to capable hands. I don't want to feel pieces of me die because I need someone. I don't want to worry that my softness will be a prospered weapon against me "someday." I want softness that frees me from staying three steps ahead so that I always have the upper hand. Because when I'm not seeking power, I can rest in my vulnerability. This is a softness that mends. This delivers us to freedom.

This kind of praxis, softness as an act of resistance and liberation, can't possibly attempt to emulate white womanhood. White women ain't ever been that kind of free in their performance of the *Cult of True Womanhood*. Hegemonic femininity—the concept that an ideal, dominant picture of womanhood exists[3]—is the buy-in of "traditional" feminine gender norms such as a sweet disposition, modesty, domestic aptitude, and includes deep investments in physical appearance and sexual attractiveness that privileges thinness.[4] Highly pervasive and exclusionary, hegemonic femininity works to maintain the status quo and functions as highly structured, normalized group behavior.[3] Even when seated in the most respected, feminized position in America—First Lady—white women who fail to relegate themselves to the domestic sphere are castigated.

The role of *First Lady* has long been heralded as the "controlling image of white womanhood that simultaneously privileges white femininity and subordinates black womanhood."[5] Like Black women's controlling images of mammy/matriarch and jezebel/sapphire, the *First Lady* image has been used to reinforce discriminatory cultural practices to uphold idealized white womanhood in America. Perfect womanhood is "white, middle class, and heterosexual, without career ambitions or political agendas, as well as avoidant of controversies."[5] Black women, however, are not afforded political agnosticism as our bodies are politicized in every way. Where white women are rewarded for domesticity, Black women are forced to embody feminine identities that leave us diametrically opposed to—and often harmed by—hegemonic femininity. As Handau and Simien note: "Although black women have worked to support their families for centuries in America, they are not stereotyped as the 'hard-working professional woman' or 'feminist' but rather as the Mammy or the Matriarch. The historical role of the [First Lady] is part of a naturalized social script constructed for the achievement of white women with the help of Black women."[5]

Privileged white womanhood is a curated kind of femininity intended to do nothing more than propagate hegemonic masculinity—the systemic creation of gender inequity in society through hierarchical masculinities (e.g., "alpha" males versus "beta" males), differential access among men to power (over women and other men), and the interplay between men's identity, men's ideals, interactions, power, and patriarchy.[6] Hegemonic femininity fails as a paragon of liberation for *any* woman, but especially for those of us who are not white, middle class, cisgender, or heteronormative. Despite *white* feminism presenting various modern femininities, the *First Lady* feminine archetype continues circulating as the gold standard of womanhood. It is why we witness white women seemingly voting against their best interest—and often against other white women like Hillary Clinton and Elizabeth Warren—every election cycle. When faced with the preservation of gendered autonomy or racial privilege, we've seen the majority of US women choose their whiteness at the expense of gender liberation time and again. They've witnessed the punitive damages of other white women whose femininity contrasts with hegemonic masculinity and are horrified. By accepting themselves as apolitical and nonconfrontational, they are rewarded with privileged white femininity, wherein loss of personal autonomy seems a small price to pay. So nah, my soft *Black* life is not intended as a request to access idealized white womanhood.

The kind of softness I speak of is what dreams of self-actualization are made of. An ethic of softness that has deeply studied and critically considered the intersections; one that has worked not to rearticulate capitalist oppression through women's empowerment brunches dressed in "hey, sis" and "divine femininity." This softness I long for dreams of a world where Black women can taste freedom as our full portion. I dream of a soft life where we do not feel compelled to conceal the full spectrum of our feelings with an armory of strength, resilience, and long-suffering. Softness that, as a Black woman, no longer restricts my life to dichotomies of having a career or receiving intimate care. I want softness that leaves room for my brokenness and does not demand resilience and guerilla warfare for survival. I am under no delusion that I can withdraw from the realities of navigating the world in my privileged and marginalized identities, but I do believe in the word of the [Audre] Lorde: "Caring for myself is not self-indulgence; it is self-preservation, and that is an act of political warfare." My aspirations of softness are a resounding rejection of the ideas of femininity that have burdened my Black womanhood. My softness is an unapologetic existence that reminds a violent, oppressive culture that I am worthy of care because I've decided to matter despite everything that I've been conditioned to believe. It is a reclamation of my right to articulate and redefine for myself a cultivated life instead of being eaten alive by the pursuit of ideals that were never formed to include a fat, Black, femme *me*.

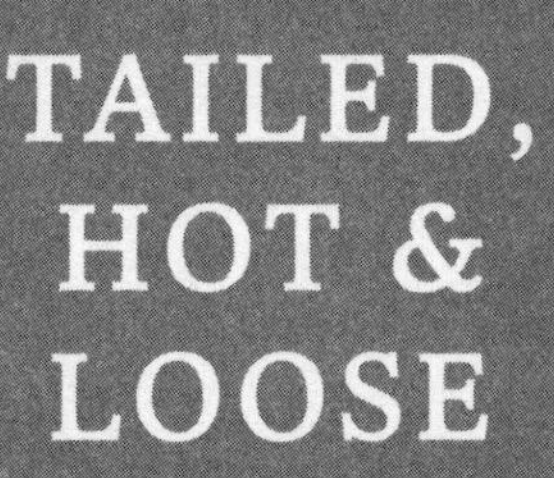
TAILED,
HOT &
LOOSE

Twerk Somethin'

First giving reverence to God
Who's the head of my life . . .

I was glad when they said unto me,
There's some hoes in this house

The story goes
Paul and Silas
Locked up in jail
Their own personal hell
Began to sing and pray
And at midnight, the doors were opened
And they were freed

Meg Thee Stallion, ridin' like the chariot swinging low
And Cardi B, doing the Lord's work
Dropped a song
At midnight no less
Where there was decreeing and chanting
Legs were open
And deliverance was available
Unto thee

When the asses gather
Begin to move in a rhythm that calls
Up and down
Side to side
There should be no question

That only the *Divine*
Can create the body that *dutty wines*

When Cash Money Records
And '99s were taking over 2000s
God, universe, and ancestors conspired
Inspired
Our hearts desires
And chose said anthem
To be the minstrel that moves us forward
By reaching behind
They taught us Sankofa
By showing us that the only way we would be moving forward
Is if we
Back that ass up

For centuries and dynasties
You've been able to find the hand of God in the movement of the body
We were taught that God was creator
Maker of the heavens and the earth
I know this to be true
Because of the evidence

You need a chance to experience heaven
Throw that ass in a prayer circle
You need to be connected to Earth
Throw that ass in a prayer circle

Don't you dare let that ole
Slew footed devil
The hand of the enemy
Has no power here
You tell that pale satan
To go back to the pits of the white supremacist hell
From whence he came

We bind the spirit of respectability
Reject the restricted gospel
And refuse to believe the lies that ain't preaching
liberation

There's healing in a twerk circle
Those are both dance, exercise, prayer, meditation,
and release

It is your divine right
Embedded in your dna
To be in a
Symbiotic relationship with your body

Well I've been before you
Long enough
And so as I come to a close
The doors of the church are opened

If there be one
Who has not gotten to know the truth for yourself

If you believed the lies that something was wrong that
God calls oh so right
If you wanna be delivered
If you wanna be healed
If you wanna be set free
If you want to move your ass with me
The altar is open
And I promise
Once you've experienced the freedom for yourself
I promise, you'll never be the same

—Valerie B

• 12 •

Ain't No Harm in Moanin'

We entered our home for the weekend, a luxurious hotel suite whose north wall of exposed brick was lined with windows overlooking busy Canal Street in the New Orleans French Quarter, flooding the room with light that bounced off the stark white walls and cerulean blue ceiling. Dropping our luggage on the floor, tastefully carpeted in a modern baroque design of cobalt blue and champagne gold, we slid exhaustedly into the white linens of our king-sized bed. Pulling in the room's blue hues, the bed was dressed with a runner embossed with the words *Sleep Saintly* on one side and *Play Naughty* on the other, the latter being something I desperately hoped to experience.

It was my thirtieth birthday and the fourth one I'd experienced with my then boyfriend. I met him shy of my eighteenth birthday after he showed up with his best friend at my church. He was four years my senior, and my romantic attraction was not immediate, but it wasn't long before we became friends. He was as *churched* as me, giving ease to our budding friendship without needing to explain what is already understood by shared experience. Our friendship was short-lived before my infatuation grew deeper. After I confessed my puppy love crush to him and his subsequent curving of my affection, life took us in starkly different directions. He started a ten-year prison sentence, and I started my undergraduate studies. We'd briefly reconnected throughout the years, but just before his twenty-eighth birthday, a mass text message brought us back into the same connection that built my romantic feelings for him before. Major life events often seemed to mark our breakups and makeups—our first romantic breakup after two years was a birthday, and Daddy's death brought us back together. Travel always illuminated the inequities between us as I footed the bill for everything while he enjoyed seeing more of the world than his resources would allow. Our relationship began with a road trip to Washington, DC, with his promises to love me, and its death knell began its toll that weekend in New Orleans in the wake of one broken promise too many.

Two months before, in another hotel suite overlooking the Atlanta skyline, we'd agreed to consummate our years-long relationship. Our deep commitment to our faith led us to mutually choose abstinence until marriage, but several years in, with no marriage in sight and my own rejection of purity culture, I pushed reasonably hard to renegotiate that agreement. In all painful honesty, I was searching for validation of our commitment in sex that I wasn't receiving in any other way. I suffered through unmet emotional, spiritual, financial, and intimate needs by trying to *unconditionally love* a man accustomed to conditions. In my attempts to be fair and amicable, I repeatedly lowered and moved my boundary lines. I sacrificed myself, my finances, and my needs repeatedly to build and support him. I hopelessly held out hope that he would see me as genuine, supportive, unconditionally loving, and worthy of giving his full self in equal return. What I received in return was my own diminishing while he continued taking everything that I gave. But here we were, in yet another self-funded baecation meant to celebrate *me*. Instead of moans of pleasure, our hotel suite would echo my guttural weeping and his laughter while berating my feelings of disappointment from another breached agreement. By the time we landed in New Orleans, I'd been begging him to meet the one need he could fulfill. I allowed him to gaslight my expressions of desire for sex to make me feel like a sex-obsessed whore. I lowered my boundaries until there were simply none left. I questioned myself instead of his intent, allowing his projections that in holding him accountable for our agreements, my sexual needs were wrong or less important than his selective moral superiority. Accessing my God-given right to sexual pleasure had been reduced to negotiations and bargaining—a cycle that started long before I met *him*.

My experience is embarrassingly common as most religious, celibate women rush into marriages to end the loneliness of abstinence while satisfying the demanding tenets of devout purity. Intentional self-denial of our natural sensual urges is motivated by the avoidance of religious guilt rather than a desire to deeply connect with one's self or anyone else. I'm not ashamed to say that I was one of those women. My ex-partner was a walking manufacturer of red flags, and I was still insistent that our relationship culminated in the *perfect Christian marriage* built on the foundation of doing it "God's way." My desire was not to say I wasted so many years of my life bound and determined to become his wife. My foolish hope in the face of being shown his unabridged true character motivated me in choosing to believe in a potential that simply didn't exist. I didn't want to be a fool—at least not more of a fool than I'd already been in my desperation for love. I wanted to believe that it would be rewarded if I did everything right and with sincerity. I didn't want to feel stupid for how much I sacrificed without payoff. And every kiss, I love you, and every promise I read between the lines for sincerity became the foundation of my faith in us until I didn't even have *pain* left to give. Even after having done everything "the right way," I was still without the symbolic trophy of *gettin' chose*. I didn't land here because of some gutless trope of a fat girl desperately paying for love or self-flagellation through devotion to emotionally unavailable people. I stayed longer than I should've because I was robbed of the knowledge that pleasure was my birthright by purity culture *and* misogyny before I was old enough to understand my sexual and self-expression. I stayed because I learned a story of God that praises endurance and long-suffering as virtues. My indoctrination of God concerning love is deeply wrapped in literal human sacrifice exemplified by the death of Jesus. I likened my building up of a broken partner to my reasonable, Christ-like sacrifice. I've prioritized partners over my needs because faith tells us that love "always protects, always trusts, always hopes, always perseveres. Love never fails." It is a belief that too often paralyzes us when our partners repeatedly demonstrate that they do not honor or value us as whole people. It's a wound that can only be healed by being willing to shift your personal narrative of God.

Purity culture is a beast complicated by the implications of race and gender. The emphasis on sexual purity, particularly the abstinence from sex until marriage, is driven by a core belief that sex beyond the confines of cisgender, heteronormative marriage is sinful. I came of age between Juanita Bynum's *No More Sheets* and Trin-i-tee 5:7's "My Body" as the soundtrack of my sexual awakening—and subsequent repression. My earliest memories of hearing sex discussed in the church are wrought with fear-based messages against premarital sex, dominated by analogies of dirty, used, and abused inanimate objects likened to our bodies. Dating was damn near out of the question given its high risk of physical contact because, let *them* tell it, even a peck on the cheek was a gateway to getting fucked seven ways from Sunday. In this world, there is no more prized capital than a woman's virginity, and we were taught to guard it with our lives, tying our worth and value to its symbolic sexual purity. The commercialization of purity movements like *True Love Waits* pushed the girls who managed to resist temptation to the top of the social hierarchy and allotted a haughty attitude of superiority for an act that was otherwise considered *tragically uncool* by the world outside the church. Purity culture is an easy market to position oneself in as a leader. The approach is formulaic and safe: abstain from sex, be blessed with a spouse for your obedience, and ride off into the sunset of God's promises. It is a well-worn marketing method with new, willing consumers each day. As long as internalized sexual shame is coupled with desperation for a spouse to be validated and made holy, purity culture will continue to be marketed (and profited from).

At home, those teachings were a convenient tool to prevent an unwanted teenage pregnancy. Mama started talking to me about sex at the age of six—a necessary discussion to explain why there was no shame in my budding exhibitionist masturbation habit, but that it was an act to be committed in *private*. Sex was never situated within shame and guilt from Mama or even Daddy, except to say it should be avoided until I was old enough to make smart decisions, but the church gleefully filled in those missing pieces. I wasn't just growing up with Christian conservatism but in the realities of being a Black woman.

Black women's sexuality has, historically, been negatively constructed and perceived. It has been positioned as oppositional to white women's sexuality while simultaneously rendered invisible and hyper-visible in dominant discourse.[1] Although Black women tend to talk more with their parents about sex than Hispanic-Latinas or whites,[2] discussion outside the realm of intercourse is often taboo. Undoubtedly, this is likely because Black America loves themselves some Jesus. We have had an ongoing affair with intense religiosity for generations. Religiosity is broadly defined as "the importance of God, frequency of church attendance, and prevalence of prayer in daily life."[3] According to a national survey, Black Americans "are, by most measures, the most religious group in the world."[4] The Black Church continues to be a community pillar as one of the few institutions built, financed, and controlled by Blacks.[5-7] Society has traditionally exercised its influence through religion to limit sexual experience to marriage.[8] Therefore, recognizing the pervasive presence of the church within the Black community, it is reasonable to assume the institution has influenced sexual attitudes—and I am no exception.

Compartmentalization, repression, and conformity have been the dominant themes of my relationship with sensuality. The pressure of performative piety has often overwhelmed any meaningful connection with sex, leaving me to experience pleasure cerebrally rather than as an uninhibited, primal instinct. The indoctrination of purity culture fares well in allowing me to hold the facade of formality while denying the unabashed feral cravings that whet my sexual appetite. Where the church praised my self-restraint, I was imprisoned by the shameful throbbing between my thighs as I lay in bed in the darkened post-meridiem hours. In between convincing myself that my body was the Lord's temple, I was tormented by the desire to be utterly defiled by the touch and warmth of another. I hungered to be fucked in ways that I pretended to be deeply offended by in the presence of others. The guilt washed over me each time I allowed my mind to wander to those illicit moments of pleasure, convinced that it was an irreparable betrayal of *His* love. In the many moments where my flesh could not be crucified by religious platitudes, the warmth of my hands became the failsafe escape that still preserved my *purity*. My arousal has been fed by almost every expression of sexuality, and there are very few *preferences* and categories that can be named that I, by my colorful imagination *or* eight to ten pages of deep scrolling, haven't *finished* from. I know *from* is a preposition, however, it is important to use here as the entire frame is colloquially for a sexual orgasm. I've begged for my intrusive thoughts of these *sinful* acts being met by God's wages of immediate death to release me, squeezing my eyes tightly to deepen my focus on my quickened breath as my fingers move deftly through my wetness. Before I can stifle the moans of my mounting orgasmic delight, I am already confessing in whispered prayers for absolution while the sticky sacrament from my pleasure ritual coats the folds of my intimacy.

I wanted so badly to be good and seen as holy and in *right relationship* with God. When we choose the Cross, we are told that we are receiving freedom, only to be shackled by oppressive theology that preys on our vulnerability. My whole life has been shaped by the persistent misogynistic belief that womanly bodies are the downfall of men, so it was a seamless transition to experience teachings that indoctrinated my body as a site of immorality and distraction—even to myself. Denying our desires, telling ourselves that sex is bad until it is made holy by marriage, and calling it salvation in hopes of achieving holiness is an opiate that goes down easily. The severance between sacred and sensual in my pursuit of holiness created a deep fissure in my *wholeness* that took years to heal.

Sexual purity is a double-edged sword that cuts *Celie* women as deeply as the *Shug Avery* ones. In Alice Walker's *The Color Purple*, Celie is our protagonist, who survives years of abuse by her stepfather and later her husband. She is quiet, submissive, and devout in her Christian faith as a respite from her bleak reality. She later befriends blues singer Shug Avery who, through the intimacy of vulnerability, helps Celie find her voice. Celie embodies all the qualities of a good, pious woman: she doesn't question the authority of others and yields her personal autonomy to their will. Her sexual experiences are limited to the confines of marriage, despite often being nonconsenting at worst and emotionally detached from pleasure at best. Juxtaposed to Celie is Shug Avery, a worldly woman with a sharp tongue and unapologetic sensuality that oozes from her very essence. Her unabashed sexual experiences earn her a reputation as a woman of questionable morality, leading to her disowning by her preacher daddy. She is the polar opposite of Celie, having decided to self-define from her lived experiences rather than having her identity imposed upon her.

Their shared lover, Celie's husband, *Mister Albert*, is equally harmful to both women despite the appearance otherwise. He objectifies Celie as less than human to create delusions of power to prove himself as a man to his daddy while objectifying Shug to validate his sexual prowess and desirability. Like *Mister*, purity culture leverages the vulnerability of women to further gendered power in favor of those who would otherwise be exposed as fraudulent. Otherwise, *Celie* girls would remain ignorant of the limitless possibilities found in the reclamation of our voice and personal autonomy. Without the nurturing of the same sexually liberated women we're taught to fear, our pleasure is left up to the whim of partners who are only vested in their *own* needs.

Emotionally, the embarrassment of having embraced this lifestyle and extolled its virtues to all who would listen, only to end in heartbreak, was not easily consoled. This was a hurt that ran deeper than past breakups. I gave a new level of vulnerability and openness to my ex because the absence of sex required it to build an emotional connection. Even without sex, I struggled with the same insecurities as in previous relationships. I dealt with the same negative characteristics in this man as I'd dealt with in other men. My trepidation of soul ties—the idea that sex creates irrevocable energetic bonds between two people—compelled me to stay where I was wholly unloved. Sexual abstinence was supposed to remove the blinders from my eyes, but instead, I bound myself to him through my fixation of holiness that the soul tie was created just as if we'd had sex. I wanted to be free from the religious guilt of shunned choices and martyred myself just for the satisfaction of having sex the "right" way. My "any means necessary" approach destroyed me emotionally and spiritually, leaving me depleted of all connection to my own sexual energy.

The ugly truth of purity culture is that not all of us get to our happily ever after and are left in the wake of incongruence in the promised reward of our faithfulness and our lonely realities. My self-perception had become so driven by the reward of sexual repression that its rejection left me in an anxious identity crisis. When such a high value is placed on the commodity of our sexuality, what becomes of us once we have sex? Becoming "like everyone else" introduces a deep-seated and complex fear in our psyche, dictating our sexual behaviors. Sexual purity is pushed as a salve for a wound that cuts so much deeper than how we engage our pleasure. It vilifies sex as the enemy of perpetually single women suffering through heartbreak instead of holding accountable the true culprit: our collective socialization of dating and relationships.

Women are bred, born, and groomed for an end game they've invariably been taught they have no choice in. Godly womanhood, especially around sexuality, teaches that a woman's objective is to be considered marriageable by a man, even if a woman doesn't *desire* cisgender men. There is a subtle assumption that the chaste

Christian woman unlocks "the cream of the crop" of available men coupled with some sort of esoteric knowledge on being a good wife. In pushing sexual chastity, how are we cultivating women to be good people? How are we helping to mold them into people who create a global impact outside of "women's business" of wife/motherhood? What does God gain through the repression of our sexuality? More importantly, how does God delight in our withheld sexual pleasure and high-risk failure of abstinence? How cruel an image we've created of God wherein we think nothing of telling people that they've created impermeable spiritual ties with those who have violated and harmed them. Further, we tell them their continued suffering is because of God's punishment.

Seven years of abstinence, mostly spent in an emotionally abusive relationship, left me raw. Physically, my own sensuality slipped away the longer I abstained from sex. Sexual arousal became so devalued for me that I struggled with the reawakening of a sexual appetite that I'd prided myself on suppressing for so many years. I struggled to reconcile my sexuality with my spirituality because I spent so many years being told that the two were mutually exclusive, the secular and the sacred demanding that I either be sexual or spiritual with no room for the *and*. Surviving the relationship was my overcoming, but there was still the matter of finding my way back to the embodiment of my sexual self. It was not enough to intellectualize sex as something normal and positive to experience. Complete reconciliation meant giving myself to experience the sex I'd finally decided was sacred.

Shortly after my breakup, I ran back to the comfort of my college sweetheart. He was a familiar lover without a learning curve, a path of least resistance that felt well suited for the job. Getting him into my bed didn't take much convincing, but our would-be tryst was abruptly interrupted by my anxieties and fears. *Well, that's not entirely true.* I was a little nervous, and I still had every intention to fuck him. But as I stood in my kitchen while he stripped in my bedroom, I heard the loudest "NO" from my spirit I'd ever heard in my life. It was like a united chorus of God, the Spirit, my ancestors, and guides in a four-part harmony demanding that I abort this mission. But I suppose saying "anxious fears" sounds a little more relatable than that.

Fortunately for me, a willing suitor was right around the corner. I'd been in a community with a preacher with whom I shared several mutual connections. Our colleagues-to-lovers pipeline was slow moving, a pace I deliberately established. Almost immediately, our professional conversations were breadcrumbed with his personal interest, but I learned long ago never to shit where one eats. Moreover, all my womanist beliefs and sexual liberation could not ignore the reality that my work as a woman in a male-dominated industry left me dancing on a tightrope between being respected and being regarded solely as another warm bed in which men could find comfort. While I considered the worst, I had to admit that his innate understanding of our shared work and the need for discretion made him a safer bet.

Risk firmly calculated, my curiosity bested me, and I responded to Preacher's suggestive messages with my own not-so-subtle innuendo. Afterwhile, we agreed to a no-strings-attached meeting in a few days. The days leading up to our rendezvous filled me with a variety of anxious thoughts about my readiness, his ability, and the potentially disastrous outcomes of this choice, but when Sunday came, so did I. He kissed away the knots in my stomach formed by the debris of shame for Sunday sexin'. As his face disappeared between my thighs, so did my apprehension that I was committing an unforgivable sin. With every stroke, he brought me back to myself and reminded me just how good it felt to be both desired and fully consumed by a lover dedicated to my pleasure. We lay in post-coital bliss, and I knew exactly what it meant to have sexual healing.

In the last several years after ending my last relationship, I've realized that if the fear of hellfire and brimstone had not intervened when it did, I would not have lost so many years in torment. I know now that I should've been better to my body. I deserved better than my self-perpetrated abuse and robbery of pleasure. I've spent almost three decades knowing just how good my body feels as climax radiates my entire being, and I *still* chose to hate myself for it. I lost years of hedonistic pleasure pretending that my love for God was incompatible with my love of sex and everything it encompasses. I'm not without my regrets from abstinence, and the years of self-denial have left me with a lament that even David couldn't write a psalm about.

In the years since my breakup, I've experienced pleasurable sex that made my eyes roll and toes curl. My body has been a respite for some seeking healing in my pleasure, but I'm still waiting for my moment to *exhale*. I am still weighed down by the social, political, and emotional nuances of what it means to have sex in *this* body. My continued healing from both religious dogma and socialization now demands sex that makes all of me feel safe, whole, and fully held.

Admittedly, this essay might be the hardest one I've written. I fought my vulnerability every step of the way. Stripping myself bare in this way is terrifying. It's one where I worry that by admitting that I, too, am subject to the human condition, I am somehow a failure. But I also know what it means to be made free by the truth. The truth is I have been imperfect, but I can still grow and recover. I can always write a new truth. My heavenly petitions are no longer to be delivered from the desires of my heart but for an exorcism from the bondage of beliefs that leave no room for the holiness of sexual pleasure. I believe God is just as concerned about my *coming* as my going and listens patiently when I speak about my desires to fulfill my sexual needs. I believe God hears my prayers for the restoration of years once eaten by the locusts of unholy religious dogma—because I've finally experienced a God who hears my moaning prayers too.

• 13 •

The "Let God Be True Quickly" Agenda

> Some people thought I was worried about all this mess when the LGBTQ or whoever they *was*, was coming after me. I told them I didn't know nothin' 'bout no LGBTQ. For all I know, it means Let God Be True Quickly! [*Speaks in tongues with an arrow-slinging motion.*] That's how I feel about that. I don't know nothin' else 'bout it.
>
> —Pastor Kim Burrell sermon excerpt (2019)

As far as agendas go, I can say that between being raised Black, Southern, and *churched*, there was no greater agenda shoved down my throat than compulsory heterosexual monogamy. And nowhere else did I witness the failings of this agenda than in the center of my moral authority: the Black Church.

If it seems like I've been in Atlanta for nearly every significant event in millennial memory, it's because I'm *really* from Atlanta, contrary to the arbitrary district lines Omeretta the Great tried to draw in her song "Sorry Not Sorry." Picture it: it's 2010 in the Hollywood of the South, and there's a theatrical production underway that only a few who were paying attention saw coming.

In 2010, four young men accused *the* Bishop Eddie Lee Long, Senior Pastor of New Birth Missionary Baptist Church, of coercing them into sexual relations with him. A lawsuit was filed, and the claim was that the bishop engaged in sexual acts with each of the men on separate occasions. The reaction was polarizing to the Black Church and the community at large—you either believed he was guilty of pastoral abuse, or you believed this was an attack of the enemy. There was no in-between. Out of my morbid curiosity, I found myself seated amongst the congregation of one of my childhood church homes, waiting with bated breath for Bishop Long to address the accusations on the first Sunday *after* the shit hit the proverbial fan.

In Atlanta, Black megachurches have territories like street gangs. The westside of Atlanta—everything after the I-20 West and 285 interchange into Cobb County toward Six Flags—is the undisputed territory of Word of Faith and Bishop Dale C. Bronner of the iconic Black hair care family company, Bronner Bros. The southside of Atlanta—everything from Old National to Fairburn—is run by World Changers and Creflo Dollar. For the *high society* Black bourgeoisie of Atlanta from downtown to Cascade, you either belong to the historic Ebenezer Baptist under Senator Rev. Raphael Warnock or Elizabeth Baptist under Craig Oliver. The Eastside of Atlanta—from *the Dec* (which shouldn't be confused with the City of Decatur) to Evans Mill Road in Lithonia—has peaceable treaties in its multiparty territory.

Saint Philip AME Church runs everything from the Candler Road Flea Market down to Memorial Drive and from Candler Road at South Dekalb Mall down to Wesley Chapel. This territory is co-run by E. Dewey Smith's House of Hope and William Murphy's dReam Center. The outskirts of the City of Decatur to North Druid Hills have always been run by New Beginning Full Gospel Baptist Church, and the Morton Brothers have maintained a stronghold in Atlanta since the '90s.

But the sprawling campus of New Birth—including the old one off Snapfinger, which is now home to Dr. Cynthia Hale and Ray of Hope—has always been a known landmark of East Atlanta from Stone Mountain to Lithonia. Put it this way: despite their sanctuary seating *thousands* every Sunday, New Birth would rent out the now defunct Georgia Dome to host its Easter and Watch Night (New Year's Eve) services, and they would still be at capacity. So basically, at some point, you could throw a rock at a group of ten Black folks and hit at least five members of *Six Flags Over Jesus*—I mean, New Birth. And there was no better time to have a season pass to New Birth than *that* Sunday.

According to the embarrassment that is my *Facebook Memories* from almost twenty years of personal data, I was apparently "amazed at how QUICKLY people take to a story" when news of Bishop Long's accusations broke in late September that year. To be honest, I had one foot in the "he's guilty" camp and the other tapping to the drumbeat of justice of yet another pastor being unfairly maligned by an *agenda*. From the perch of my soapbox, I admonished people who couldn't be paid to "pass on the WORD of God, but [they] QUICKLY share gossip" to remember that "Bishop Long's sins (or the lack thereof) won't get me into heaven or keep me out of hell." I wasn't interested in defending Bishop Long for his innocence but instead launched a self-defense campaign against the onslaught of damaging claims against the church. I told you, church membership is much like reppin' one's set in a violent street gang. Instead of bullets, we assassinate lives with butchered Bible verses to condemn to hell every*body* that is neither straight nor cisgender. In this culture, an attack on one of our leaders is an attack on the entire body. Because yo' *pastor* is as much of a personal identity as your chosen faith.

I *got saved*—that is, I came into a personal relationship with Christ—at nine years old. During a Wednesday night Bible study, Rev. (now Bishop) Jackie McCullough preached and I felt the call. I'd only known church my whole life, as my dad was a preacher and my mom kept me in fellowship. But that night, I felt the call and tug at my heart and decided to seek my own relationship with God. I found God at New Birth, and, for that reason alone, it will always be significant for me. Maybe it wasn't just morbid curiosity that drove me back into the sanctuary that Sunday but also a nostalgic love I held that powered the tenuous hope that the accusations weren't true.

That morning's atmospheric energy felt like what I imagine happens at Trump rallies. I arrived early anticipating the increased turnout on *top* of the normally high-traffic worship services at the Lithonia, Georgia, main campus. The pews didn't take long to fill with parishioners *and* spectators. The vibe was high, and the camaraderie among us was strong. Eponymous chants and campaign signs were replaced with an *us versus them* attitude. As you'd expect, the presence of national media was treated with great suspicion. But regardless of what side of the aisle you stood, we were all palpably eager to hear the *truth* straight from the horse's mouth.

After the pomp and circumstance of praise and worship, the moment we'd been waiting for arrived. Bishop Long walked his *green mile* to the podium hand in hand with his long-suffering wife, Lady Vanessa Long. It was the expected optics of a well-planned crisis management strategist that we've seen time and again: undoubtedly broken and embarrassed women being asked to play the Tammy

Wynette "Stand by Your Man" role beside their embattled husbands as they prepare to sell the public on their innocence.

Finally, he addressed the audience: "I've been accused. I'm under attack," he began in solemn earnest. He continued, "I want you to know, as I said earlier, I am not a perfect man. But this thing, I'm gon' fight." The applause in the sanctuary was thunderous and immediate. He had spoken the words we'd all hoped to hear, affirming our confirmation bias that there was no way *our* leader had done what they *said* he did. This was indeed another attack that had to be valiantly fought.

"And I want you to know one other thing," he began again while waiting for the crowd to settle again. "I feel like David against Goliath. But I've got five rocks, and I haven't thrown one yet!" And with that, he dropped the mic and exited stage left, leaving behind a thoroughly captivated, cheering crowd of committed supporters.

In the exodus from the sanctuary to the parking lot, people carried with them the self-satisfaction of *I told you so*. Car horns blared in solidarity and intimidation of the few protesters gathered outside during service. The troops had been rallied, and thousands that day were ready to join Eddie L. Long on the battlefield against the *gay agenda* to destroy a *man of God*. For me, though, that Sunday morning moved my feet from a split stance to a firm opinion: Bishop Eddie Long was guilty of what he'd been accused of, and that realization changed *everything* for the grace and fleeting hope I'd once held. I had to reconcile my own internalized homophobia *as well* as the failure of my moral authority to, well, act morally.

Long's abuse survivors—Anthony Flagg, Maurice Robinson, Jamal Parris, and Spencer LeGrande—reportedly buried the matter for an undisclosed amount in a settlement one year later in 2011. Centino Kemp, a fifth accuser, came forward as the lawsuit entered the mediation process. He, too, settled for an undisclosed amount soon after. In 2017, Bishop Eddie Long succumbed to a long battle with cancer at sixty-three, leaving behind a complicated legacy of healing *and* harm.

Bishop Long's lasting impact is the raising of a ministry that thrived on homophobia and the oppression of LGBTQIA+ identities. While I hesitate to label or hypothesize about his sexuality, Bishop Long became a victim of the very same homophobic, patriarchal culture he helped to incubate. There are, undoubtedly, countless young queer Christians who were browbeaten by his theology. His fall came at the hands of the very thing he so powerfully preached against. I firmly believe that he preached so fervently against it due to his internal struggle. Regardless of the truth of the accusations against him, he helped to create an environment that was not conducive to allowing him to be unapologetically authentic.

Homophobic patriarchy is partially responsible for how quickly people latch on to child abuse accusations of pastors. Bishop Long stood accused, tried, and convicted only in the court of public opinion. While we must take stories of survivors seriously, we must also acknowledge our hypocrisy. Homophobia enables us to believe same-sex abuse with limited proof. Homophobia enables the murmuring that the cause of death for Bishop Long was HIV/AIDS because of the probability of sex with men. Patriarchy allows the justification of abuse by men against women. Homophobic patriarchy collides to silence sexual abuse in a way that is nearly impossible to surmount. I can't help but imagine that had Long's accusers been young women, he might have retained similar men's success, support, and dignity.

Homophobic patriarchy is why, despite video footage and repeated violations, R. Kelly was still selling out shows before his 2019 arrest and subsequent conviction in 2021. He is still being denied the apt title of child molester while being defended at every turn. Homophobic patriarchy is why Cosby's fifty-plus accusers have had their survival stories dissected, dismissed, and denied in dominant public opinion. Men berated women for not wanting to support the theatrical production of two accused rapists when *Birth of a Nation* was released. Nate Parker was, despite proof, upheld and exonerated by many of the same tongues wagging in fiery anger toward Eddie Long. I remain wholly unconvinced that gracious defense would remain if even ONE of the victims of the aforementioned men had been another man or teen boy.

> Anybody in the room who is living with a homosexual spirit, beg God to free you. If you play with it in 2017, you'll die from it. If you play with it in 2017 in God's house, you'll die from it. Y'all came to hear about carnal; I came to tell you about sin. That perverted homosexual spirit is a spirit of delusion and confusion, and it has deceived many men and women. And it has caused a stain on the body of Christ. That perverted homosexual spirit . . . You as a man, you open your mouth and take a man's penis in your face, you are perverted. You are a woman and will shake your face in another woman's breast, you are perverted. And those homosexual spirits have been angry, and they come up against you [saying] "you gotta love everybody." Sit down, you serpent.
>
> —Pastor Kim Burrell, sermon excerpt (2017)

I've often joked that you can take us out of the church, but you can't take the church out of us—*us*, in this instance, meaning both the individual person and our collective cultural narratives. The vast and sweeping influence that the Black Church has had as the cornerstone institution of Black folks cannot be denied—or excised. Its customs are deeply entrenched among us regardless of individual religious affiliation. If you started a call and response of *God is good all the time* in a room full of Black folks of all walks of life, I guarantee you they'd all intrinsically know the proper response: *and all the time, God is good.*

I have witnessed homophobia grounded in biblical exegesis from Black folks who decry Christianity as a self-destructive opiate. Our ideas of gender roles and norms are drenched in white supremacist tropes and made holy by the insistence that *God's word don't change*. Much like its customs, the religious ideology of the church is so enmeshed within our cultural narrative that its dogmatic adherence is sustained even in the absence of faithful participation. It is not enough to simply leave the church without disavowing these narratives.

> There is an unspoken synergy between black women and black gay men; an understanding of how their plights at many times intersect and create naturally-formed bonds based on their lived experiences within the context of patriarchy and hyper-masculinity. Black women who have spoken against LGBTQIA-identifying people only expose the hard truth: there's much work to do to reconcile these often broken relationships between black women and their same-gender loving counterparts. Though it's trendy to have a gay BFF on social media, black women don't always show up in droves when it comes time to stand up against the violence and oppression of black gay men."
>
> —George Johnson for theGrio (2017)[1]

I don't believe that Black folks are any more homophobic or sexist than any other ethnicity, but that we are products of our cultural conditioning. Cisgender heterosexual Black women have an appropriative at best and terse at worst relationship with Black gay men. By and large, we've co-opted the language of Black gay ballroom culture and claimed it as our own. We seek out gay men to *beat* our faces and *slay* our hair. Yet, in all of this, we have no problem gaining our liberation at the expense of these same men. Somehow, their humanity becomes blurred by our vision of queer identity and culture as merely a trend to assimilate into our own.

More than what Burrell says in her homophobic sermonizing is the vigor with which she says it. There is a distinct, unique malevolence in her tone and body language—one that I find all too familiar. It embodies a distinct personal bitterness dressed in scriptural interpretation. It is easily dismissed as standing for the kingdom instead of a red herring of vitriolic projection from a personal wounding. It claims to preach in tough love but with good intentions to bring us all closer to holiness. It is the kind of religious mindset that cleaves to a "love the sinner, hate the sin" ideology. Healthy love is not given in fragments; we cannot love people in pieces. "Love the sinner, hate the sin" treatment of LGBTQIA+ identity is merely the cousin of "the sin was in the sex, not the baby." The same Bible we cleave to as a bat against our gay brothers is used to shame and berate us as well.

We often blame the existence of queer men for our singleness, consoling ourselves with the false belief that we'd be happily coupled otherwise. We put them on the altar of sacrifice in our churches so that we may seek elevation within religious patriarchy. We ostracize effeminate Black gay men as trying to "be us" while we parrot the culture they've distinguished for themselves. Our relationship with LGBTQIA+ folks, especially Black gay men, is quite similar to race relations between the dominant race and minority identities. We happily benefit from the good while drawing a distinct line in the sand at the viewing, treating, or defending them as our comrades in the fight against the oppression that crushes us all. The antagonism between us is not one-sided, however. Not by a long shot.

Black gay and queer men who continue to uphold sexism and patriarchy stoke the ire in our fragile relations. To be clear: gay men can (and often do) participate in misogyny. We are beholden to the objectification and criticism of our appearances by queer men as much as we are by straight men. In our churches, we are criticized for everything from our hairstyles to our failure to wear the proper undergarments. Gay male culture has decided to, in its own way, define how womanhood and femininity should be presented. And, unlike with straight men, it's not even born out of sexual attraction to our bodies. It is purely from their power as men to assert dominance over our bodies and tell us, as men, how we can better exist as women. I'm not sure if the chicken or the egg came first. That is to say, I don't know if we (Black women) antagonize them (Black queer men) because they started it or vice versa. I do know that it is, at this point, an exhausting game of tit-for-tat that serves neither of us.

Black women are more similar than dissimilar to Black gay men in how we experience oppression both external to and within our community. In the church, neither of us experiences healthy sexual dialogue or liberty. We both struggle to reconcile the beauty of our sexuality with the tenets of our faith. We're both told by the church to suppress our sexual desires. Both of our sexualities are often blamed for the fall of otherwise "upright and upstanding men." We're both welcome to serve and lead auxiliary ministries for as long as our sexualities remain closeted and repressed. Yet all too often, when given the opportunity, cishet women will join the chorus of oppression of Black LGBTQIA+ lives in Jesus's name.

In the way our queer siblings are berated, cishet Black women are told by their churches that the fruit of our womb is shameful because it was not conceived in marriage. Then we're told that the sin was in our decision, not the production of that decision. We then spend nine months to a lifetime trying to atone for what we've been taught is an egregious error. We seek repentance in rushed, loveless marriages. We seek reconciliation through denial of ourselves. We seek atonement at the expense of others' liberation. The sexualities of cishet women and gay men are all too often fodder for shame and exploitation within the church. When will we see the parallels between ourselves? When will we recognize that we all want our identity and sexuality to be respected and reconciled? Both groups within the faith and beyond the church want nothing more than to be whole. But be clear: the liberation, equality, and respect of Black women, particularly in the church, should not and will not come at the expense of Black queer folks. Our wholeness can only come through the transformation and renewing of our mindset.

The church is often blamed for passivity in the Black community. We blame the church for collective ignorance. We blame the church for community poverty. We blame everything but white supremacy because somewhere inside, even when one leaves religion, Black people are still blamed for their oppression. We still act as if we did something to incur the wrath of hegemony. This idea that if people weren't religious, they'd aggressively pursue their liberation is bunk. We have plenty of nonreligious Black folks and have made little to no traction with full liberation. Because while religion is a tool of white supremacy, it is not the source. Yet, like salt, *Black Jesus* is in everything that makes up our enculturation of

Blackness. Like white supremacy, our cultural agreements of homophobia, sexism, classism (even as subtly as respectability politics), and other antagonism of marginalized people are well maintained even without a church membership. Thus, its overt *death-dealing* through maintaining these hegemonic practices and beliefs as holy must be transformed at the source.

How do we move forward? Well, the church has to first accept itself and say, "We have done harm, and it is time for us to make recompense to those we have done harm." To do this, we must unpack how the Black Church places marginalized bodies—specifically femme and queer bodies. We've got to admit that we normalized, through our cultural agreements and theological truths, that these bodies are to be seen but not heard unless they're entertaining or comforting us.

I grew up with and under the direction of brilliant choir directors whose queerness was closeted by plexiglass. I also grew up with my Uncle James, my daddy's *very gay* best friend, and Uncle David, my daddy's *very gay* end-of-life caretaker. All of these men *deeply* loved God and the church even though it refused to love them back beyond their utility in service. I witnessed Daddy lend his heteropatriarchal privilege to protecting these men from his place in the pulpit. Still, churches that would happily call Uncle David to cater a grieving family's *repast* wasted no time preaching against his "sinful lifestyle" the following Sunday. On the contrary, my dad's *hetero whoredom* was never met with rebuke and became little more than shop talk amongst the brotherhood of the cloth. Yet, most of our discourse around same-gender-loving people often begins and *ends* with sex.

There are two active dynamics of oppression happening here. First, there's the active misrepresentation that queer identity is *only* about sex. By doing so, their identities are easily made salacious.

Because we are in sanctuaries and communities that already sensationalize and demonize consenting sex between unmarried hetero folk, of course, we will do the same to queer bodies to further emphasize the "perversion" of their existence. This requires forcing sexual experience in a dichotomy where if it doesn't fit within the conditions of heteronormativity, we assume that the *only* difference that matters most between us and our siblings that are *openly* same-gender loving (SGL) is the sex. Secondly, our tendency to center same-gender-loving-people's sexuality with the sex part speaks to our inability to have honest conversations about sex. When I say *ours* in this context, I want to be clear that I am talking about cisgender heterosexual people. My tendency to romantically partner with men despite my attraction to women, *too*, drives my self-inclusion. It's not as much a personal bi-erasure as a recognition of the privilege of being hetero-presenting.

Because our cultural conditioning has left us with many puritanical hang-ups around our own sex lives, we filter our internalized discomfort through restricted behavior codes for *all* of us. The church does not have real discussions around pleasure—full stop. Sexual conversations in our churches are often rooted in self-denial and rejection of the body, sexuality, and sensuality. Because we don't have honest conversations about our own bodies and our own pleasure, we project those same ideas onto other bodies whose sex doesn't look like ours. In many ways, the church's willing obtuseness in ignoring the *love* between queer bodies also shrouds our ignorance of what it means to be fully inclusive and have healthy conversations about love. To speak honestly about what it means to love and to have consensual loving relationships between SGL people also forces us to admit that much of the dialogue we have in church about what it means to love is rooted in power dynamics where one person or one gender has to have *less* power and *submission* to be fully loved. To acknowledge queer bodies as being about more than sex forces the rest of us to grapple with if this *love* that we've espoused ourselves to have for the "sinners" among us mirrors the type of love that we're commanded to have by the scriptures or if this love reflects back to structural disenfranchisement that we have created and sustained.

The *body* language of the church when it speaks of same-gender-loving bodies is almost as ugly as what it communicates verbally. We see folks get a little *stiff* in their bodies at first sighting, followed by the knowing looks passing between people when someone walks in our sanctuaries who is visibly queer. We hear the "loving" call for deliverance in the casual ad-libbed lyrics of our favorite gospel songs. The worst part is that we do not see this language as violent. We see it only as a reflection of our statement of faith, relying on what we believe the Bible has said about queerness. The reality is that we're literally telling people to *come out* of what God has called them *into*. The idea being communicated is that queer bodies are not *holy* enough to be called or covered by God. We take God's intention into our own hands, deciding that these identities conflict with what we've interpreted the Bible to mean about their personhood. It is an insufferable arrogance to deny the humanity of LGBTQIA+ people on the argument that "God doesn't make mistakes." When God created people, people introduced restrictive gender and sexuality rules to that already perfect creation. These rules are meant to concentrate dominion and power in the hands of a few at the expense of the whole. Our hubris in suggesting that LGBTQIA+ identity defies God—not just our arbitrary sexuality and gender constructs—is nothing short of audacity.

Despite constant abuse at the hands of its churches, nearly half of all US LGBTQIA+ folks still identify as Christian, with a nearly even split between Protestant and Catholic—neither of which are open or affirming denominations.[2] What has persisted is no matter what narrative man has projected to be from the heart of God through Bible-based homophobia and antagonism, the heart of God is still compelling people to come from the highways and hedges and be in community. It's compelling them to find spiritual places that are safe, sacred, and that see them as already holy. The church's theological distance between this reality and its rejection of the *Let God Be True Quickly Agenda* exists because we do not want to reconcile that perhaps the texts of terror that we've used to justify our homophobia require us to actually deal with uncomfortable truths. The passages of Leviticus 18:22 and 20:13 do not prove that we should pray away the gay. These verses refer to cultic prostitution, not loving, consenting relationships. They're part of a long list of Jewish laws, most of which are not followed by Christians today—because Lord knows I'm probably responsible for keeping the *seafood boil bag* industry in the black despite Levitical codes against shellfish. Sodom and Gomorrah were not destroyed because *people be gay* but because of violent sexual assault. If we skip to the New Testament, I Corinthians 6 and I Timothy 1 are not proof texts for homophobia. The [assumed] author of both books, Apostle Paul, was likely talking about male prostitution and pederasty, a socially acknowledged romantic relationship between an adult male and a younger male usually in his teens in Ancient Greece. Romans 1:26-27 doesn't prove what the other scriptures fail to prove about #TheGays, either. Cultural context matters. Paul didn't understand gender like we do today. More importantly? Paul uses this to lead into his argument against idolatry as a sin, not gay folks. While the church has strived to make LGBTQIA+ identity an ULTIMATE "sin," the Bible often lumps it in with other issues like corruption, greed, gossip, and idolatry. The word *homosexual* didn't even appear in English translations of the Bible until 1946.[3]

Maybe we should focus less on trying to make consensual intimacy a sin (spoiler: it's not) and more on the sin of systemic greed that dehumanizes Black, Brown, queer, disabled, and "othered" bodies.

A time of reckoning is the leading item on the agenda that we can no longer table until the next meeting. The church has preached love as we created a culture of hate and intolerance. We remained far too silent when we knew abuse was taking place at the hands of our church leaders. We inadvertently taught families to protect the abuser and shun the victim. We helped to fan the flame of homophobia in the Black community. We asked people to deny their truth and the fullness of their being. We say so much about love but often fail to do enough to *actualize* love for people whose lives complicate our narratives and force us to deal with the structural inequity we sustain.

The church has delighted in being both the sole arbiter and adjudicator of our morality. However, it now shies away from the mirror that reflects an institution that has often held itself above reproach. The queer, gay, trans, and lesbian *stones* that the church builders once rejected are now the rocks crying out to make both their harm *and* calls for accountability known. If it is to continue as part of the Black future, the church has to reckon with itself how it has failed to be a site of liberty and justice for *all* Black lives.

· 14 ·

Catchin' the Heauxly Ghost

THE MOST TALKED-ABOUT PERSON in the Black Church after Jesus, Paul, and 'em is probably Beyoncé Giselle Knowles-Carter. The multi-hyphenate creative frequently serves as sermon fodder with her liberal self-expression and a devoted fan base whose size rivals even the largest congregations. Having already been accused of blasphemy from many pulpits, the release of her twerk anthem "Church Girl" made church *folk* mad as hell. Even the writer and performers of the song's primary sample, "Center Thy Will" by The Clark Sisters, were called to rebuke and denounce the work. Under the guise of *elder privilege* to "speak out, say something" in observation of harm, Bishop Patrick Wooden Sr. called the work *sacrilege* and a piece of trash before suggesting that not only was Beyoncé not saved, but that she had, in fact, sold her soul to the devil. Given the extensive history of misogyny in the Church of God in Christ—especially against the Clark women, including matriarch Mattie Moss Clark—this is not surprising. What is even less surprising is that women pastors, whose position in the pulpit is constantly in flux and debate of appropriateness, joined the chorus of religious condemnation.

Self-anointed prophetess Tiphani Montgomery pejoratively renamed the performer *Baalyoncé*—from Baal, the Canaanite-Phoenician god of fertility and rain often used as a synonym for false gods. Montgomery sermonized the singer's fanbase as a witch's coven and prayed for violent rebuke and punishment of Christians who attended her concerts. When confronted with her hypocrisy in old tweets where she praised Beyoncé, Montgomery defaulted to the age-old claim that this devotion was before her Christian conversion. Despite the continuous state-sanctioned assault against Black lives, homelessness and hunger, sexual violence in our sanctuaries, and the costs of pantry essentials spiraling out of control, church leaders have an unnatural obsession with ensuring we see a Black woman as a *demonic force* in our community.

It seems that Beyoncé's most egregious sin is daring to be free in her Black body *without* seeking permission from others—and possibly modeling to millions of other Black folks how to do the same.

Beyoncé isn't exactly a textbook church girl. Her story doesn't include finding her voice in the choir stand or straying from the straight and narrow toward the allure of *worldly* ways. She's never shied away from loving God out loud, but she's never told us about Vacation Bible School or tarrying for the Holy Ghost. In the absence of our usual markers for identifying one of our own, it's easy to dismiss her as merely cosplaying a culture to which she doesn't explicitly belong. To do that, though, we'd need to lie to ourselves about how much the Black Church influences *Black* culture.

Beyoncé did not need to hold a faithful membership to any congregation to inherit the complex identity politics for Black churched women. This is a woman who sings self-empowering notes about the curvaceousness of her body in "Bootylicious" and shames others with that *exact same* but more scantily clad body in the next track, "Nasty Girl," on the same album. Her scathing rebuke is that so-called nasty girls make it difficult for women like herself to walk with integrity, self-respect, and dignity. As a church girl myself, it is difficult to discern if these are song lyrics or a Women's Day sermon. Teenage Beyoncé, who proudly chastises the *Nasty Girl*, will embody her aesthetic as twenty-five-year-old Beyoncé in "Freakum Dress" five years later, beginning a public journey toward emancipation.

Through her artistry, we witness a woman finding her way home to her body. We witness someone who doesn't curse publicly until 2008 as a matter of respectability, a decade into her career and only done while in character as Etta James in Cadillac Records, become the woman whose records have required explicit advisories and radio versions since 2013's eponymous digital release. In 2016, she shattered all illusions that she's lost touch with her own Blackness or the implications thereof in the "Formation" audio-visual release. In a time where Blackness could cost her every carefully curated part of her image, she doubles down instead. She stops soothing concerned church folks by adding gospel medleys for the album close. She no longer needs a safe space to project her risqué behaviors and has released the *Sasha Fierce* avatar.

Beyoncé self-actualizes into a fully integrated "Grown Woman." A woman who honors the God of Abraham, the crowning energy of Oshun, *and* the ancestors on the wall who put her *on game*. She stopped putting ten tracks of space between singing about taunting her man's other woman and her love of God. Now, she *shakes them tig ol' bitties* right over Twinkie's masterful work on a Hammond B3. Over the span of twenty years, we watched a Black woman get *free* in real-time. For those who benefit from oppression, Beyoncé is a terrifying playbook.

> My relationship to the Bible is one of love, respect, and deep wrestling along with fierce defense when I see it used in public as a prop. I question the adequacy of the doctrines of inerrancy and infallibility, showing the prominent way in which Christianity steeped in white supremacist authoritarianism responds to being called out.
>
> —DR. ANGELA PARKER, *IF GOD STILL BREATHES, WHY CAN'T I?* [1]

Make no mistake: the criticisms of Beyoncé by the church writ large are grounded in white supremacist biblical authoritarianism in interpreting the meanings of scriptures. Christianity convinces its adherents to choose accepted creeds without thinking about who and what defines them as acceptable. By positioning the Bible as incapable of being wrong (inerrant) or making mistakes (infallible), we are taught to see the scriptures as God-breathed and nonnegotiable. As Dr. Parker names:

> Inerrancy and infallibility as tools of white supremacist authoritarianism limit humanity's capacity to fully experience God's breath in the biblical text. Regardless of whether we identify as Black, African, African American, white, Asian, Latinx, or Indigenous, we have all had aspects of white supremacist authoritarianism take up residence in our minds and bodies. What will we do to remove it?[1]

Biblical inerrancy is how King David became revered for his defeat of Goliath, his role in the lineage of Jesus, and being a "man after God's own heart." As a tool of white supremacist authority, this inerrancy asks women to ignore the predatory misogyny of David in his sexual assault of Bathsheba and the subsequent killing of her husband. Biblical infallibility is how gender identity becomes fixed as cisgender male and female based on the creation mythology in Genesis. White supremacist authoritarianism in biblical interpretation praises Job for his patience and demonizes his wife for her righteous anger in having lost all her children in an inexplicable tragedy.

Authoritarianism requires that our empathy be framed not from the lens of our lived experience but from the perspective most beneficial to authority figures. What liberation would we experience if we read that text not from the position of infallibility but from our lived realities as parents, women, or marginalized people? What if we reinterpreted the "god" in Job 2:9, where Job's wife suggests he curse God and die, as ruling authorities who abuse their power? How much differently would we interpret her words if we read them from the reality of our marginalization of gender, race, ability, class, or sexuality? What would it mean to no longer suffer in silence under abuse as an act of integrity and instead decide to curse *that* god to find true freedom?

When deconstructing faith practices and religious ideologies, I am often asked why I lead with sexuality. It is for the same reason that the saints were whipped into a frenzy when they heard the call to *drop it like a thottie* over sampled cries unto the Lord to be centered in the will of God: to oppress someone, you must sever the connection between their spirit and their flesh by making them believe the two exist in permanent opposition.

The foundational interaction between white supremacist authoritarianism and the Bible is to disassociate us from the lived experiences of our bodies. Biblical inerrancy is how nonmarital sex becomes the embodiment of sinful flesh and, under supremacist authority, how we enter the toxic cycle of desiring and denying the pleasure of the flesh and calling it holiness. Religious faith rooted in and nourished by supremacist authoritarianism requires the severance of the sacred and sexual. It is an act of self-dehumanization within social structures that already limit the recognition of marginalized bodies as fully human.

Reconciling sex as a sacred, bridging experience between God and ourselves invites us back into our bodies. Within embodiment, we realize that our imago Dei, or image of God, means that our sexual desire *and* pleasure are also in likeness to God. Here is where sex ceases as beleaguered sin and becomes an intentional experience that our bodies know desire, arousal, foreplay, intercourse, orgasm, and *rest.* It becomes obvious why despite our guilt-ridden conscience, we still find ourselves crying out in uninhibited pleasure and *praise* for divinity that is bigger than ourselves in the throes of sexual passion. Once we accept that sex is both a healthy *and* holy thing, it becomes painfully obvious why "the enemy of God is relentlessly committed to fouling both immanent pleasure and transcendent joy."[2]

These realizations trouble our long-held beliefs in the authoritative teachings about not only our sexual selves but every other *infallible* and *inerrant* creed we've not questioned before. I start with sex because finding sacredness within our *whole* selves is where the journey toward a liberated faith begins.

I'd argue that Beyoncé invites *Church Girls* to come home to our bodies. *Renaissance* opens with the declarative affirmation that she will not be stopped by her detractors. She emphasizes that neither her identity nor her worth can be defined by external factors. This reminds us that holiness is ours, not by our achievement but by our birthright. Most of us have not experienced holiness that we didn't have to labor and deny ourselves for. As the album continues,

Beyoncé exhibits more comfort in her imperfections. She asks us to tally the costs of gaining the world that we were taught matters most. The world where we define ourselves by our jobs, our marital status, our haters and detractors. A world where we do not make decisions grounded in our joy but based on who others believe we should be. What Bey calls *soul-breaking* is what Jesus calls the *profit* of gaining the world and losing one's soul.

By the time we reach "Church Girl," she declares that in releasing ourselves from the stigma attached to our bodies, we open ourselves to love more. She reminds us that we are born into freedom before we were ever placed into the captivity of religious dogma and toxic theologies. Beyoncé invites us to experience revival through *Renaissance*. She uses the familiarity of Black musicianship and oration to seamlessly usher us into unfamiliar freedom. She mirrors the beauty of celebrating the tension, dichotomies, and divinity of relying on Black memory alone as wholly sacred.

Hearing a twerk anthem over one of my favorite gospel songs felt like an indulgent rebellion, maybe even a bit like a guilty pleasure of a forbidden coexistence between the sacred and the secular. In the group chat, my homie Acharo said,

> It's the liberation for me. It's ownership, agency, and autonomy of one's humanity. It's the dismantling of restrictive religious dogma that served only those that forced it upon us. It's the LIFE that we've all felt deep inside but caged ourselves in due to respectability politics. It's the power to be and know you are whole. These are some of the things that I get from that track. I'm not a diehard BKC fan, but this song has given us [the] power to be unapologetically and beautifully human.[3]

A messenger that inspires freedom is terrifying to those who profit from pandering captivity as salvation. The church has profited from a gospel that asked us to find peace in our brokenness—and Black women have paid an astronomical sum. As my sista-friend Nancy chimed in,

> Too many words, experiences, and evils have turned a lot of Black women into the walking dead. Beyoncé is trying to bring us back to life! *Renaissance* is a defibrillator for our hearts, our soul, and our emotions. That's why Bishop [Patrick] Wooden [Sr.] is so mad. The walking dead pays tithes, goes to all those patriarchal COGIC conferences, and listens to church garbage year after year. I am tired of being a member of the walking dead![3]

> "I regard authority as a "living" and "breathing" conversation. However, what many of us fail to understand is that conversation is always mutual."
>
> —DR. ANGELA PARKER, *IF GOD STILL BREATHES, WHY CAN'T I?* (2021)

I imagine we've reached the "what about what the Bible says" point of our conversation. I will not ask you to abandon the scriptures altogether, but I will invite you to consider the lens through which you've previously understood them. Our understanding of these scriptures is often through a charismatic evangelical perspective. This perspective makes biblical authority fixed—unable to be challenged as wrong or mistaken. It is a perspective that leads us into bibliolatry: a pejorative term used to describe the practice of focusing so much attention on the Bible as a book to be venerated and idolized that the fact that it is divine revelation from God transmitted through human authors is overlooked.[4] This practice often obscures other important issues in the text and ignores the intricacies of our faith.[1]

We are suffering from a loss of conversation partners. With fixed biblical authority, we do not treat our interactions with the sacred text as an ongoing conversation between past testimonies, present experiences, and hope for the future. Instead of being in conversation with, we have been preached to and kept immature in our faith and beliefs as a result. Fixed authority presents the Bible as equivalent to God, while fluid authority recognizes the Bible as a mediator of God's presence. A fixed perspective of "God-breathed" interpretation will never allow for the necessary challenge of discerning the diversity of voices in the biblical text. White supremacist authoritarianism in scriptural interpretation has always been in the tradition of "minimizing Black people's actualization of our God-given, inspired breath—our authenticity and authority."[1] How we read the scriptures and their authority matters.

"But the Bible Says . . ."

If you've ever been close to church culture, you've undoubtedly heard the story of Ruth and Boaz. It is taught as a model of God's love for us and focuses on the tragic losses of Naomi and Ruth with the death of their husbands, cleaving to one another, and the ultimate faithfulness of God to bless them both through Ruth's marriage to Boaz.

Ruth is given to Christian women as an example of how to carry oneself during courtship. This story—and the culture attached to it—plays on the long-held suspicions of the body and pleasure.[5] In the Christian faith, sexual pleasure is suspicious by default and, if not carefully controlled, becomes incompatible with a godly life. It is a restrictive relationship wherein pleasure is depicted as ultimately unfulfilling for its own sake. Since sexuality is a part of the body, the original site of sin, it is irreparably dirty. It forces us to choose between the "sinful" pursuit of carnal pleasure or true lasting joy.

In Ruth 3:1-5, she is instructed to put on her *freakum dress*, find Boaz, wait until he passes out drunk, then uncover his "feet" and lie down with him and wait for him to tell her what to do. In case it isn't clear to you yet, "feet" is a biblical euphemism for genitalia. Feet is used in the same context within these verses in the book of Genesis: a polite way to describe male genitalia. In the Hebrew text, especially Old Testament context, it is often cited that this word [feet] is an idiom for male genitalia. In context, the *piel* verb that translates to the English "uncover" is generally used in the context of illicit sexual acts. This idiom, however, is *not* carried over in the New Testament, where we see plenty of foot washing.

As Tod Linafelt puts it:

> Boaz is clearly half-drunk and half-naked when he awakens to find Ruth lying next to him. Who is this woman, Boaz wonders? How far have things gone? With Boaz in a state of confused vulnerability, Ruth offers herself to him ("spread your cloak over your servant," Ruth 3:9). She tells Boaz that he is the "next-of-kin"—the man in a position to redeem ownership of Elimelech's property since there is no male heir. That is, Ruth sets things up so that if Boaz wants her, then he must also help Naomi economically, thereby also giving Boaz a cloak of respectability with which to cover his romantic interest in this foreign woman, an interest suggested in Ruth 2:5

> and confirmed in Ruth 3:10. Boaz, though vulnerable and confused during the nighttime meeting with Ruth, turns confident and effective in the daylight, as we see him publicly implement Ruth's plan (Ruth 4:1-6).[6]

A more fluid authoritative reading of these scriptures offers not only a destigmatized perspective of nonmarital sex, but it also invites us into a conversation with the culture of the text. Without social agency within a patriarchal society, Naomi guides Ruth into what is effectively survival sex work. Unable to work, own property, or otherwise provide their own financial stability because of their gender, Naomi instructs Ruth to seduce a drunken Boaz through oral sex. In conversation with our own ethics and the evident culture of this sacred text, this exchange between Ruth and Boaz also brings tension about sexual consent. Fixed, supremacist scriptural authority has not allowed us to focus on these intricacies in the name of inerrancy and infallibility.

This passage invites us to reconsider our association of sex and punitive spiritual consequences. We have been taught to equate our holiness, our marriageability, and our salvation to what we do with our bodies. It is a harmful practice that separates our sexuality and our spirituality while robbing both of fullness, meaning, and passion. It is an invitation to question the emphasis of supremacist authoritarianism that gender subservience is a natural, biblical order. Judah and Tamar's story in Genesis 38 offers a similar invitation.

Judah and Tamar are in a complex and intriguing relationship. A fluid authoritative read of these passages depicts a narrative of sexual agency, empowerment, and the pursuit of justice. In the story, Tamar, who was married to Judah's oldest son, becomes a widow. According to the cultural practices at the time, Judah's second son, Onan, should have married Tamar to fulfill his duty as a brother-in-law. However, Onan refuses to do so and practices a form of contraception, which ultimately leads to his own demise. Tamar, left without a husband or any prospects for marriage, takes matters into her own hands. She disguises herself as a prostitute and waits for Judah on the road. When Judah approaches, he mistakes her for a sex worker and propositions her. In this act, Tamar exercises agency and takes control of her sexuality, seeking to fulfill her desire for a child and secure her future.

Tamar trades sex with Judah after failing to become pregnant by his three sons. Tamar negotiates with Judah and asks for a pledge, which she later uses as evidence to hold him accountable. This demonstrates her resourcefulness and determination to ensure justice and secure her rights. It portrays her as an active participant in her own sexual life and highlights her pursuit of her own needs and desires.

The issue in the text isn't the sex. It's Judah's lack of integrity. The fact that he had sex with her and that she used sex to teach him a lesson cannot be read that something is wrong with sex itself. Tamar's actions challenge traditional gender roles and expectations, emphasizing her autonomy and ability to navigate societal constraints. There is liberation in reading this passage from a perspective that recognizes Tamar's sexual agency, her empowerment in pursuing her desires, and her quest for justice within the confines of her societal circumstances.

No matter what your favorite sermon says, Song of Solomon (Songs) is not an allegorical book of poetry about the passion of Christ and the church as His bride. *Songs* is a book about passionate intimacy between lovers—full stop. Its inclusion as a canonical book of the Bible means its contents have been determined as sacred and accepted as true. If we believe that the Bible is a holy and sacred book, that must also include the sacred holiness of the eroticism found in the Song of Solomon.

Song of Solomon 5:2-6 expresses desire, longing, and the beauty of sexual intimacy between two lovers. The imagery used in the passage is symbolic and sensual, evoking a sense of anticipation and passion. The speaker awakens to the sound of their beloved knocking, representing the initiation of an intimate encounter. The repeated use of endearing terms like "my sister," "my love," and "my dove" reflects the deep affection and closeness between the two individuals. The description of the beloved's head being wet with dew and locs with the drops of the night suggests a physical exertion or excitement, adding to the sense of sensuality.

The speaker, already prepared for bed and having bathed their feet, hesitates to get dressed again, highlighting their eagerness to embrace the intimate moment. As the beloved attempts to enter, the speaker's heart is thrilled, signifying their emotional connection. The mention of myrrh, a fragrant resin often associated with love and intimacy, further enhances the sensual tone of the passage. However, there is a moment of disappointment when the beloved turns and leaves. The speaker's soul fails them; they actively seek their beloved, calling out for them. This could symbolize the longing for emotional and physical connection, emphasizing the importance of open communication and mutual desire in a sexual relationship.

This sex-positive perspective appreciates the passionate and intimate nature of the passage, highlighting the desire, anticipation, and longing between two lovers. It emphasizes the importance of emotional connection and open communication in fostering a healthy and fulfilling sexual relationship. Most importantly, it treats the pursuit of pleasure as both sacred and worthy.

No biblical discourse about the relationship between sexuality and Christianity is complete without unpacking the baggage of the apostle Paul. Paul's letters to the church at Corinth have long served as the rubric for sex and the good Christian. It's not that Paul is wrong; our reading of this letter as anything other than exclusive to Corinth causes trouble. *All* of Paul's letters are written to "specific Christian communities regarding specific issues that confronted those assemblies of believers."[7] Without the historical context of the sociocultural norms that impact these scriptures, we can't have full conversations about what Paul says. Paul is writing his opinions based on his belief in the imminent return of Christ in his own lifetime, and from his own baggage. Paul's hyper-religious devotion to the Christian faith is in no small part his own attempts to nullify the effect of his role as a former persecutor of the church. Simply put, Paul's extensive discussion on sex in 1 Corinthians is because he felt that sex was a distraction from preparing oneself for the return of Christ. For Paul, there was no greater cause to devote oneself to than the Second Coming.

Paul's most revered sex commentary is 1 Corinthians 6:9-10: "Do you not know that wrongdoers will not inherit the kingdom of God? Do not be deceived! Fornicators, idolaters, adulterers, male prostitutes, sodomites, thieves, the greedy, drunkards, revilers, robbers—none of these will inherit the kingdom of God." For centuries, pastors and congregants have treated these verses as self-evident truths while ignoring what is lost in translation. *Pornos*, translated in this verse as a fornicator, is a male prostitute. The sodomite, translated from the Greek *arsenokoites*, is indeed same gender sex but usually denotes a man who tends to sleep with boy children—a pedophile. "Male prostitutes" in this passage is translated from the Greek *malakos*, which describes *soft* or effeminate men. It is a designation for any man who doesn't fit stereotypical hegemonic masculinity—irrespective of their sexual preference. As Michael J. Brown notes, "All of these behaviors would call into question a man's masculinity, at least according to Roman social norms. The malakos is the man who is a public entertainer, who is overly concerned about his looks, cannot control his desires, [and] allows . . . the softening of his manhood."[7] In other words, cultural norms we extol as virtuous would be seen as effeminate in the days of Paul.

Paul's condemnation of sexual desire is his belief that all the named behaviors in these verses prove a lack of self-control and discipline. This is a Paul who preaches against sex work but not about masters who sleep with the enslaved—a cultural norm as prominent as prostitution. He even ignores that many prostitutes are *also* enslaved persons with no bodily autonomy. Paul doesn't even have all the answers for the Corinth church, much less for future societies whose lives and customs are starkly different than his own. We've built entire theological frameworks on the words of someone who saw sex as nothing more than a utility for procreation at *best*. We're attempting to live according to the urgency of a thirty-five-year life expectancy in Paul's ancient Rome when our own is more than double that at about seventy-three years. Worse, we've built Christian sexual ethics grounded in patriarchal ideas about masculinity *and* absent women's sexual agency.

> Most Black Christians have been indoctrinated to bifurcate their bodies and their spirits, and have a tendency to use the Bible as a sort of twisted security blanket to support these antiquated ideologies. It is the external mistreatment of our temples that convinces us that we need to internally disassociate from our bodies.
>
> — LYVONNE BRIGGS, *SENSUAL FAITH: THE ART OF COMING HOME TO YOUR BODY* [8]

The result of inheriting a supremacist biblical authority is our development of spiritual anxiety about what we do with our bodies while ignoring what is done *to* our bodies. Pastor Lyvonne suggests that *salvation* in the Bible is intended to be understood as *healing* rather than a ticket out of hell.[8] Healing is an intentional, consenting choice. Healing must include the reclamation of all parts of ourselves as holy—including our sex—to be made whole by our salvation.

Many pulpits have profited from our dysfunctional relationship with our living, breathing, pleasure-seeking flesh. Unsurprisingly, reclamation of our bodies and sexual autonomy from the clutches of manipulative structures is labeled as heresy. Those invested in our brokenness will gaslight us otherwise when our healing disrupts their harm against us. If we cannot get free in our bodies, we will struggle in vain to find liberation elsewhere.

I know this conversation feels sacrilegious to some. Our indoctrinated beliefs about sex leave little room to witness these words as anything more than a corruption of scripture to support a personal agenda. I struggled to work out my own soul salvation in the disruption between the sacred and sensual. Every shedding of a new layer of my theological paradigm raised my awareness of buried fear and trepidation. I pushed through my resistance because I was tired of living in an unholy war with my body. I was tired of feeling inadequate because of uncontrolled desires that religion told me were abnormal. I couldn't utter any more empty prayers to be delivered from my sex drive. Fasting, tarrying, crying, and pleading with God to be freed from lust only left me with an increased awareness of the sexual needs of my body. The lesson of these unanswered prayers made me draw a single conclusion: God did not need to deliver me from sexual desire to make me holy. I am holy, inclusive of my sexuality, not despite or in denial of it.

> In this here place, we flesh; flesh that weeps, laughs; flesh that dances on bare feet in grass. Love it. Love it hard. Yonder they do not love your flesh. They despise it. This is flesh I'm talking about here. Flesh that needs to be loved.
>
> —Baby Suggs, *Beloved* by Toni Morrison[9]

Maybe your journey is similar to my own. You participated in church communities that taught pleasing God required denying your body the pleasure of touch. You were saddled early with the burden of wanting holiness so badly while always feeling you'd never be enough to have it. Your longing for God to be pleased with you was seemingly unrequited. Perhaps you see your body as defiled for merely existing and desiring the experience of loving lust. You've spent nights begging desperately to be delivered from the iniquities of your sexual self. Unlearning years of religious rhetoric of self-repression is not easy for *any*body.

Throughout this text, I've offered theories that may provide you a location for healing,[10] but it may still take considerable time and work to move from information to informed *practice*. One of my favorite spiritualists and scholars, Jade T. Perry, describes the exorcism of patriarchy-disguised-as-spirituality:

> Once I allowed myself to have a sexual life, I was voracious in my appetite for the theory that would somehow make it feel all-right. It felt like maybe one day the right string of words would unlock something in me. Perhaps it would take away the fear of everything that was assigned to a Black church girl who was having premarital sex.[11]

The key to liberation is not merely knowledge but an unshakeable *knowing*. Knowing can only come through embodiment—the experience of living in and connecting with our physical bodies. Embodiment returns our awareness to the body's sensations, emotions, and movements. Our bodies are not just vessels that carry us around; they are integral parts of who we are. Embodiment allows us to recognize the wisdom and intelligence of our bodies. Hunger, fatigue, pain, and pleasure all signal what we need for our wellness. Listening to and honoring these signals lead us to choices that support our overall well-being.

Although the body is always with us, we've been preached into a constant dissociation with it. We cover it modestly in our churches. We shame it privately in mirrors that reflect our deepest insecurities. We punish this flesh into submission of whatever we need it to be—thinner, more muscular, lighter, or darker. We treat our flesh as insubordinate, a disobedient entity needing constant discipline. Yet, this body matters so much to God that the incarnation of divinity happens through *human flesh*. John reminds us that "the Word became flesh and lived among us" (John 1:14). If God trusted flesh and blood enough to manifest the incarnation of Christ through it, why are we so distrusting of our own flesh made in God's image? Who or *what* benefits from the hermeneutic of suspicion in our *own* tendons, ligaments, and bones?

This is an altar call to come home to *your* body and study the war between sensuality and salvation no more. You were born free to experience good touch without religious guilt. The way home begins with giving yourself permission for both pleasure and desire. Honoring our erotic, sensual, sexual selves is paramount to our collective well-being and freedom. Our healing, joy, resistance, and liberation from oppression will *always* be a *worthy* thing.

Always a God Thing

Every moment that you felt out of sorts
For feeling at home in your body at good touch
It was a God thing

Every time you couldn't figure out why you didn't quite fit
in the places you were supposed to belong
It was a God thing

Every meal that brought you joy
Every minor chord that brings a needed presence
Every roll on your body
Every piece that made you queer
Every hair on your head in *those colors*
And every time you changed them because you felt like it
It was a God thing

Every time you built a wall to survive
And hide who you truly are
And every time those walls were torn down
Because the true you emerged anyhow
It was a God thing

When you revealed yourself
As pro-Black
As sci-fi lover
As African spiritualist

As loud
As vegan
As horny and willing to do something about it
As cosplayer
As astrology lover
As pro-choice
As loud
As obnoxious laugher
As introvert
As ambivert
As full, whole, intentional being
We are apologetic no more
We perfect as is
We are not *a wretch undone*
We are not *worthless filthy rag*
We were never *original sin*
We were loved from jump
We were
We are
We will always be
A God thing

Now go in peace
And *sin* some more

—VALERIE B

Valerie Boyer is a minister, poet, vocalist, musician, dancer, activist, historian, and educator. Born, raised, and groomed in the southern hospitality of Galveston, TX, her life's work reflects the southern colloquialisms of her childhood and the tenacity of her adulthood. Her words and poetic voice breathe knowledge into every space, inspiring all people to show up as full selves and create the world they want to see. She is a proud Howard University alumna and can be found on all social media at @vrbeeee.

GRATITUDE & RECOGNITION

God of my youth, thank you for anchoring and preparing me.

God of my weary years and silent tears, thank you for being a promise keeper.

Jehova, ke tshepile Wena.

To my venerated ancestors and descendants to come, thank you for choosing me. I am honored to heal, lead, and initiate on your behalf. I pray that my life brings y'all honor and joy.

Thank *you*. Yes, YOU, friend! Thank you for every word, paragraph, and page you just read. Thank you for going through every hope, fear, and joy that immerses my story. You didn't agree with everything, but you gave me a chance anyway, and I cannot express my gratitude enough. Thank you for your trust and your support; it means the world to me.

Rebekah Borucki, aka Prez BexLife (lol): in our acquisition meeting, the first thing you told me was that you *loved* the title of my book. What you didn't know was how *nervous* I was that I'd need to change the title to be publication friendly. Yet you expressed both love and admiration for a title so audacious in a world that often kills women like me for it. It was at that moment that I knew Row

House was the place I wanted my work to call home. Thank you for truly believing in raising the volume of voices that matter every single step of the way. Thank you for trusting in my audacity.

My friend and editor, Tamela Julia Gordon, this book wouldn't have escaped the basement of my Google Doc outlines without you. From the moment you invited me to the Row House table, my life hasn't been the same. The first thing you told me was to trust my voice and expertise *first* before relying on the words of others as more valid than my own. Your words have become my leaning post in this whole process. I am honored to be so well loved by you throughout this journey. Thank you.

aunjanue, my friend and foreword author: Your brilliance is one of my favorite indulgences. When I prayed and asked God who needed to be the first voice readers witnessed, the answer was always you. I wanted a voice who, as you so eloquently named, shared my scars and understood my tears. I will never not be grateful for your enthusiastic answering of my call. The world may still be catching up, but I'm grateful for the privilege of already knowing just how much you are *that* girl. Love you immensely!

There are a host of friends, family, and communities who have all supported me in the writing process. Be it patience for my limited time, grace for my frustrations and neediness, or shared excitement about it all, this work couldn't be without each of you. I didn't grow up with a large community of extended relatives, but I've been adopted and well loved by a host of Black folks along the way. Thank you to all the aunties, uncles, mamas, cousins, and grandmamas who've chosen me as family and loved me well. **Special showers of love to my sibling and Bonus Mom!**

While my love for my people, culture, and identity started at home, I must give deep gratitude to the spaces where it matured and flourished: the Department of Africana Studies at Georgia

State University—special shout-outs to Drs. Jonathan Gayles and Akinyele Umoja who never let me slack, no matter how smart or beloved I am! Thank you to Alonzo A. Crim Center for Urban Educational Excellence as well—Drs. Susan Crim-McClendon (ibaye) and Brian Williams, Bryan K. Murray, and colleagues-turned-homegirls Shaila P. and Alex C.

LeVoyd Carter, I have benefited from your legacy twice as a product of the Department of Africana Studies and as a DEI Professional. You held space for me and saw my professional best when others did not. I couldn't have survived that season of my life without you. May your soul continue to rest in complete peace.

Thank you to those whose work, words, and lives have nourished my wisdom and intellect. Especially those whose names I called on in the birth of this work: Toni Morrison, Fannie Lou Hamer, Audre Lorde, Ella Baker, James Baldwin, Malcolm X, Kwame Ture, James Cone, Katie G. Cannon, Albert Cleage, Kinitra Brooks, Brittney Cooper, Angela Davis, Patricia Hill Collins, and countless others encountered in my years of learning.

Thank you to all the journalists, podcasters, curators, planners, organizers, and others who have spoken my name in rooms where I've yet to enter. My visibility has never been a one-woman show. I am here because you saw something worthy in my work, and I'm eternally grateful.

Shout-out to my comrades & co-conspirators in the work: Candace Y. Simpson & Rev. Mama Emma Jordan Simpson, Lyvonne Briggs, Whitney Baisden-Bond (Rev. Motha), Jade T. Perry (Auntie Muva), Kristian A. Smith, Donnell McLachlan, Amber Louisa Lowe-Woodfork (Revvun Ambuh), Rev. Dr. Neichelle Guidry (love you *DEEP*), Melva Sampson, Erika Gault, and all who know that justice and liberation are the end goal.

Ruthie & Zach, y'all are still my favorite melanin-redacted people, *lol*, and I'm super grateful for the beautiful loving friendships I've built with y'all. Ruthie, you have blessed me in more ways than you'll ever know. Thank you for loving me sincerely.

RXB & Linda, there are no words to capture my gratitude for you both. You welcomed me into your home and hearts. From dinners to celebrations and all the LIFE in between, your love for me has never faltered. I'm honored to know and love you both! TMFH—we're in this for *life*!

People/Spaces that hold me up AND down: Dr. Tony McNeill (love you DEEP), Jugga Levert (JG), The Pastor's Study (TT), the Unfit Christian Congregation, Kamala Miller, Candace Boyd Simmons, Imani Wilson, Dominque Pollard Adams, JoLondon Smith-Givens, and all of my friends in the DMs across my social platforms—your words of levity and encouragement carry me through. Thank you!

Every couple that bestowed me the honor of officiating your marriages, I hold each of you dear to my heart. *Kim & Shaquinta*: I love you both in such a special way. Beyond allowing me to marry you, y'all have faithfully loved and supported me every step of the way in this work. So proud to know and love you!

Time and again, I've found God and my salvation through Black women. For the Black women who have provided me spiritual care, nourishment, and uplift: Tynia Johnson-Anderson and Keka Araújo (Okún Sérèfí Oní Yemayá), my thanks is woefully inadequate for the ways you pray for me, affirm me, and cover me. Y'all have spoken over my life, given me respite when I wanted to quit, and called this very work into being on my behalf. Thank you for seeing me as worthy.

My therapist, Dr. Andreka Peat: I would not be here without your healing. You empowered me to take my liberation and trust my instincts. You held space for me, and you taught me how to be aware of my breath and to know myself as worthy. You are my favorite therapist, and my gratitude runs over for the five years we spent together.

Chantell and Jeralyn: I love you both real bad! I've made so many memories with y'all that I treasure. I'm grateful for your love and support at a moment's notice. Thank you for letting me love your children as an auntie and godmommy. To have held and watched your babies grow has been an honor. Thank you for the bonds of sisterhood for over twenty years!

My sistas-in-love from the group chats: Raven D., Eboni P., Dani S., and Jen H.—Y'all have watched me grow since the age of twenty. Over a decade later, I'm grateful each of you is only a message away for anything I need. My Baes (Chrishele, Lex, and Sharie), we've been through astounding highs and lows together, but I couldn't have done this without the encouragement and support y'all consistently provide. Thank you!

Sistafriends who've been absolutely invaluable to me: LáDeia Joyce, Erika R., Nontombi (Naomi), LaJanee, Mia (Mickey Mack), Joan Nicole, Rae Nelson, Tiff Tuck, Tenia B., Dominique Mack, Tati Richardson, Kim McCarter, Nneka Onuorah, BossLady Davone, my cousins Janae and Jada B., NaTasha Chantell, Cortnie Lorelle, Leah De Shay, and dozens of others. Love y'all!

For women who taught me to embody an unapologetic aesthetic of myself, I hope I'm doing you proud. Though there are many, there are a few I'll name: Queneesha Monique, Nita B., Brittney A. G., Dr. Lindsay B. (LuxATL), and Tia Omodara. Each of you walk this world unafraid of your truest self. You inspire me to always do the same. Thank you.

There is something about being loved by men who do so with intention to heal, not hurt, you. I'm so grateful for the men I call my brothers. *My beloved TLT, my brother and my friend.* The watcher and the keeper. Man am I glad this work existed to connect us for a lifetime. I get on your nerves sometimes, but you are truly the best big brother I could've asked for. You love me for me, you ride for me, and, most of all, you trust me. Love you real deep!

Mike R., there are no adequate words to express my gratitude for what you have healed in me. You really, truly have had my back, no questions asked, in ways only a brother could. You believed in me in ways that I didn't even trust myself. I'll never stop thanking you for literally saving my life. I'm so grateful to know you, Favorite!

Mrs. Lanette, thank you for sharing your husband with the world. I know that the best of him is because of you. Thank you for loving me so much. You are one of the most incredible women I've ever met. And you introduced me to eggnog pound cake made with pure love! LOL! Thank you for being you!

Jamaal S., look at the world we've built from the days of @KingAmel14 and @danigirlstar. The lives we spoke into being so many years ago are now here before us. There are no words to describe love for over twenty years of being my day one. Hateretha, we did it! LOL

Brodes, my beloved Bro P. There is not a trigger, anniversary, or birthday that has passed that I do not miss you. I play old videos sometimes just to hear your voice. You believed in every part of my work that has even gotten me to this moment. I wish you were on this side to see it. Thank you for trusting me.

Valerie, what an honor it is to do life with you. You are everything I could ever ask for in a sister and best friend. You make vulnerability, trust, and love a worthwhile investment with the highest yielded returns. From now until infinity, it's always gon' be you for me!

Bonus Dad, You have loved, protected, and provided for me in ways that you were not obligated to do. You are one of my biggest cheerleaders and supporters. There is so much to thank you for, but what matters most is my gratitude for the way you take care of Mama. I never have to worry about her because I know she's in good, capable hands. Thank you, always!

Daddy, it never gets easier in your absence. There is not a grand moment of my life where I have not longed for your witness of it. I hope you are as proud of me now as an ancestor as you always were in this life. I know I'm living in the reality that you prayed for me before I even knew how to pray for myself. I love and miss you always.

Mama, all that I've ever needed, your hands have provided. You are my miracle worker, promise keeper, and ever present help in the time of trouble. Thank you for cultivating the writer, dreamer, storyteller, and fighter in me. You are my constant, my soul inspiration, and my *raison d'être*. Everything I do is in gratitude for all that you are to me. Thank you for wanting me, choosing me, and pouring every good thing into me. I love you beyond space and time. Always.

WORKS CITED

CHAPTER 2: White Man's Religion

1. Fields, Jessica, Martha Copp, and Sherryl Kleinman. 2006. "Symbolic Interactionism, Inequality, and Emotions." *Handbook of the Sociology of Emotions*, edited by Jan E. Stets and Jonathan H. Turner. New York: Springer: 155–78.
2. Cottom, Tressie McMillan. 2019. *Thick: and Other Essays*. New York; London: The New Press.
3. Barnett, Michael, and Raymond Duvall. 2005. "Power in International Politics." *International Organization* 59(1): 39–75. doi:10.1017/S0020818305050010. ISSN 0020-8183. JSTOR 3877878. S2CID 3613655.
4. Mofokeng, Takatso. 1988. "Black Christians, the Bible and liberation." *Journal of Black Theology* 2(1): 34-42.
5. Brooks, Kyle. (@ThaNubianPrince). 2016. "Jesus is on the throne. He was also on a cross. The hope of divine security doesn't negate material, deathly consequences. Remember that." Twitter. November 9, 2016. 11:37 a.m. https://twitter.com/ThaNubianPrince/status/796391315042922501.

CHAPTER 3: The Preacher's Kid

1. *Room* 222. 1972. Season 3, Episode 14. "Where Is It Written?" Directed by Charles R. Rondeau. Aired January 14, 1972, on ABC.

• • •

CHAPTER 4: Do Black Lives Matter to God?

1. Cone, James H. 1997. *God of the Oppressed*. Maryknoll, NY: Orbis Books.
2. Tooley, Michael. 2021. "The Problem of Evil." *The Stanford Encyclopedia of Philosophy* (Winter 2021 Edition). Edward N. Zalta (ed). https://plato.stanford.edu/archives/win2021/entries/evil/>.
3. Gallup, Inc. 2012, December 24. "In U.S., 77% Identify as Christian." Retrieved May 14, 2018. http://news.gallup.com/poll/159548/identify-christian.aspx.
4. Machado, D. L. 2010. "Capitalism, immigration, and the prosperity gospel." *Anglican Theological Review* 92(4): 723.

CHAPTER 5: Black & Ugly as Ever

1. Knust, Jennifer. 2014. "Who's Afraid of Canaan's Curse?: Genesis 9:18–29 and the Challenge of Reparative Reading." *Biblical interpretation* 22(4-5): 388-413.
2. Matthews, Victor H. 1994. "The Anthropology of Slavery in the Covenant Code." Bernard M. Levinson (ed.). *Theory and Method in Biblical and Cuneiform Law: Revision, Interpolation and Development*. JSOT Supplement Series 181; Sheffield: Sheffield Academic, pp. 119–35.
3. Sambol-Tosco, Kimberly. 2019. "Slavery and the Making of America. The Slave Experience: Religion | PBS." Thirteen.org. https://www.thirteen.org/wnet/slavery/experience/religion/history.html.
4. Tanner, Kathryn. 2019. *Christianity and the New Spirit of Capitalism*. United States: Yale University Press.

CHAPTER 6: Will There Be One?

1. Pobee, John S. 1979. *Toward an African Theology*. Abingdon Press.
2. Wormald, Benjamin. 2015. "U.S. Public Becoming Less Religious." Pew Research Center's Religion & Public Life Project. November 3, 2015. https://www.pewresearch.org/religion/2015/11/03/u-s-public-becoming-less-religious/.
3. Pew Research Center. 2015. "America's Changing Religious Landscape." Pew Research Center's Religion & Public Life Project.

May 12, 2015. https://www.pewresearch.org/religion/2015/05/12/americas-changing-religious-landscape/.

4. Pew Research Center. 2009. "A Religious Portrait of African-Americans." Pew Research Center's Religion & Public Life Project. Pew Research Center's Religion & Public Life Project. January 30, 2009. http://www.pewforum.org/2009/01/30/a-religious-portrait-of-african-americans/.
5. Jackson, Jenn M. (@JennMJacksonPhD). 2022. "Black memory is a form of disruption. It's a weapon not just because of efforts to erase it. But, also because it is precise. It is accurate. It is a catalogue of what we want to remember least." Twitter. August 12, 2022. 8:08 a.m. https://twitter.com/JennMJacksonPhD/status/1558062751381176324.
6. Jackson, Jenn M. 2022. "The Militancy of (Black) Memory." South Atlantic Quarterly 121(3): 477–89. https://doi.org/10.1215/00382876-9825933.
7. Public Broadcasting Service. 2019. "This Far by Faith. Denmark Vesey | PBS." Pbs.org. https://www.pbs.org/thisfarbyfaith/people/denmark_vesey.html.
8. Public Broadcasting Service. 2019. "Africans in America/Part 3/Nat Turner's Rebellion." Pbs.org. https://www.pbs.org/wgbh/aia/part3/3p1518.html.
9. Trible, Phyllis. 2002. *Texts of Terror: Literary-feminist Readings of Biblical Narratives*. United Kingdom: SCM.
10. Taylor, Keeanga-Yamahtta. 2016. *From #Blacklivesmatter to Black Liberation*. Chicago: Haymarket Books.
11. Copper, Emma. 2020. "Anything but Christian: Why Millennials Leave the Church." Medium. October 23, 2020. https://emmacopper.medium.com/anything-but-christian-why-millennials-leave-the-church-ccae210dfb06.

CHAPTER 7: "The Enemy Is in the House Tonight"

1. Simien, Justin (director). 2020. *Bad Hair*. Hulu. NEON. 1 hr, 43 min. https://www.hulu.com/movie/bad-hair-eb67f592-fd7a-4d0b-aa82-6fef5ee0dd6b.

CHAPTER 8: If Jesus Don't Fix It, the Hoodoo Lady Will

1. Easterling, Paul. 2016. "The Ifá Diaspora: The Art of Syncretism, Part 2—Santería and Lucumí." *Afrometrics*. December 2, 2016. http://www.afrometrics.org/africana-religious-studies-series/the-ifa-diaspora-the-art-of-syncretism-part-2-santeria-and-lucumi.
2. Pobee, John S. 1979. *Toward an African Theology*. Abingdon Press.
3. Hinderer to Venn. Nov. 15, 1864: C.M.S. CA 2/049
4. Cesaire, Aimé. 1948. *Introduction to Victor Schoelcher Esclavage et colonisation*. Paris: Presses Universitaires de France, p. 7.
5. Jacobs, Claude F. 1989. "Spirit Guides and Possession in the New Orleans Black Spiritual Churches." *The Journal of American Folklore* 102(403): 45–67. https://doi.org/10.2307/540080.
6. Kaslow, Andrew J., and Claude Jacobs. 1981. *Prophecy, Healing, and Power: The Afro-American Spiritual Churches of New Orleans, A Cultural Resources Management Study for the Jean Lafitte National Historical Park and the National Park Service.* Department of Anthropology and Geography. University of New Orleans.
7. Du Bois, W. E. B. 2008. *The Souls of Black Folk*. United Kingdom: OUP Oxford.
8. Newman, Chris. 2018. "Conjure, Hoodoo, and the Cross: African Spirituality and the Slave Experience in Pre-Antebellum America." *The Journal of Undergraduate Research at Ohio State* 8.

CHAPTER 9: Between Juanita's Sheets

1. Miller, Brandi. 2018. "Opinion: Patriarchy Has Found a Home in the Pulpit." HuffPost. HuffPost, March 25, 2018. https://www.huffpost.com/entry/opinion-miller-patriarchy-church_n_5ab797a0e4b008c9e5f83c77.
2. WOMAN THOU ART LOOSED, ed. 2022. "About WTAL—Woman Thou Art Loosed." Woman Thou Art Loosed. 2022. https://wtal.org/about-wtal/.
3. Bynum, Juanita. 1999. "Juanita Bynum—'No More Sheets.'" Website Video, 2018. YouTube. https://www.youtube.com/watch?v=sGCmsETc0bg.
4. Lerner, Gerda. 1986. *The Creation of Patriarchy*. United Kingdom: Oxford University Press.

5. Long, D. Stephen, and Rebekah L. Miles. 2023. *The Routledge Companion to Christian Ethics*. Taylor & Francis.
6. Chatters, L., J. Levin, and J. Taylor. 1992. "Antecedents and dimensions of religious involvement among older Black adults." *Journal of Gerontology* 47(6): 269–278.
7. Mattis, Jacqueline. 1995. "Work(i)ngs of the spirit: Spirituality, coping and the construction of meaning in the lives of Black women." Dissertation Abstracts.
8. Mattis, Jacqueline S. 1997. "Spirituality and religiosity in the lives of black women." *African American Research Perspectives* 3(2): 56–60.
9. McKay, Nellie Y. 1989. "Nineteenth-century Black women's spiritual autobiographies: religious faith and self-empowerment." In Personal Narratives Group (eds.). *Interpreting Women's Lives: Feminist Theory and Personal Narrative*. Bloomington: Indiana University Press.
10. Cone, James H. 1985. "Black Theology and the Black Church: Where do we go from here?" In Milton Sernett (ed.). *Afro-American Religious History: A Documentary Witness*. Durham: Duke University Press.
11. Dazey, Margot. 2021. "Rethinking respectability politics." *The British Journal of Sociology* 72.3: 580–593.
12. Moore, EbonyJanice. 2023. *All the Black Girls Are Activists: A Fourth Wave Womanist Pursuit of Dreams as Radical Resistance*. Row House Publishing.
13. Masenya, Madipoane. 2004. "How worthy is the woman of worth?: rereading proverbs 31:10–31." *African South Africa* 4. Lang.

CHAPTER 10: The Men All Pause

1. Boyd, S. 2011. *Black Men Worshipping: Intersecting Anxieties of Race, Gender, and Christian Embodiment*. United Kingdom: Palgrave Macmillan.
2. Butler, Judith. 2011. *Gender Trouble: Feminism and the Subversion of Identity*. United States: Taylor & Francis.
3. hooks, bell. 2004. *We real cool : Black men and masculinity*. United Kingdom: Routledge.

CHAPTER 11: Soft, Heavy & Black

1. Welter, Barbara. 1966. "The Cult of True Womanhood: 1820–1860." *American Quarterly* 18(2): 151–174.
2. Perkins, Linda M. 1983. "The Impact of the 'Cult of True Womanhood' on the Education of Black Women." *Journal of Social Issues* 39(3): 17–28.
3. Schippers, M. 2007. "Recovering the Feminine Other: Masculinity, Femininity, and Gender Hegemony." *Theory and Society* 36(1): 85-102.
4. Walter, Carly. 2020. "Is This 1920 or 2020: The Effects of Hegemonic Femininity on Diversity . . ." Association of Fraternity/Sorority Advisors, February 2020.
5. Handau, Megan, and Evelyn M. Simien. 2019. "The Cult of First Ladyhood: Controlling Images of White Womanhood in the Role of the First Lady." *Politics & Gender* 15(3): 484–513. https://doi.org/10.1017/s1743923x19000333.
6. Jewkes, R., M. Flood, and J. Lang. 2014. "From Working with Men and Boys to Changing Social Norms and Reducing Inequities in Gender Relations: A Paradigm Shift in Prevention of Violence against Women and Girls." *The Lancet* 385(9977): 1580–1589.

CHAPTER 12: Ain't No Harm in Moanin'

1. Hammonds, E. M. 1999. "Toward a Genealogy of Black Female Sexuality: The Problematic of Silence." J. Price & M. Shildrick (eds.). *Feminist Theory and the Body*, pp. 93–104. New York, NY: Routledge.
3. Hutchinson, M. K. 2002. "The Influence of Sexual Risk Communication Between Parents and Daughters on Sexual Risk Behaviors." *Family Relations* 51(3): 238–247.
4. Pattillo-McCoy, M. 1998. "Church Culture as a Strategy of Action in the Black Community." *American Sociological Review* 63(6): 767–784.
5. Gallup Report. 1984. "Religion in America."
6. Drake, S., and H. Cayton. 1945. *Black Metropolis*. New York: Schocken.

7. Frazier, E. F. 1974. *The Negro Church in America*. New York: Schocken.
8. Nelsen, H. M., and A. K. Nelsen. 1975. *Black Church in the Sixties*. Lexington: Univ. Press of Kentucky.
8. Woodruff, J. 1985. "Premarital Sexual Behavior and Religious Adolescents." *Journal for the Scientific Study of Religion* 24(4): 343–366.

CHAPTER 13: The "Let God Be True Quickly" Agenda

1. Johnson, George. 2017. "Kim Burrell and the Complex Relationship between Black Women and Gay Men." TheGrio. January 4, 2017. https://thegrio.com/2017/01/04/kim-burrell-and-the-complex-relationship-between-black-women-and-gay-men/.
2. The Williams Institute, UCLA. 2020. "More than 5 Million LGBT Adults in the US Are Religious." Williams Institute. October 8, 2020. https://williamsinstitute.law.ucla.edu/press/lgbt-religiosity-press-release/.
3. phillips, adam nicholas. 2015. "The Bible Does Not Condemn 'Homosexuality.' Seriously, It Doesn't." Medium. July 16, 2015. https://medium.com/@adamnicholasphillips/the-bible-does-not-condemn-homosexuality-seriously-it-doesn-t-13ae949d6619.

CHAPTER 14: Catchin' the Heauxly Ghost

1. Parker, Angela N. 2021. *If God Still Breathes, Why Can't I?* Black Lives Matter and Biblical Authority. United Kingdom: Wm. B. Eerdmans Publishing Company.
2. Allender, Dan B., and Tremper Longman. 2014. *God Loves Sex : An Honest Conversation about Sexual Desire and Holiness*. Grand Rapids, Michigan: Baker Books, A Division Of Baker Publishing Group.
3. Personal correspondence with Ancharo Smith and Nancy Jones
4. Patzia, Arthur G., and Anthony J. Petrotta. 2002. *Pocket Dictionary of Biblical Studies*. Downers Grove, IL: Intervarsity Press.
5. Williams, Mariam. 2017. "The Ruth-Boaz Myth and the Hard and Fulfilling Work of Being Free—#SFS17 Day 2." Redbone Afropuff

and Black GRITS Faith, Feminism, Family—from the Perspective of a Black Girl Raised in the South. August 5, 2017. http://www.redboneafropuff.com/2017/08/05/the-hard-and-fulfilling-work-of-being-free-sfs17-day-2/.

6. Linafelt, Tod. 2016. "Ruth." *Bible Odyssey*. Society of Biblical Literature . March 29, 2016. https://web.archive.org/web/20221204125035/http://www.bibleodyssey.org/en/people/main-articles/ruth.
7. Brown, Michael Joseph. 2022. "An Inconsistent Truth: The New Testament, Early Christianity, and Sexuality." Josef Sorett (ed.). *The Sexual Politics of Black Churches*. New York: Columbia University Press.
8. Briggs, Lyvonne. 2023. *Sensual Faith: The Art of Coming Home to Your Body*. Convergent Books.
9. Morrison, Toni. 1987. *Beloved*. Vancouver, B.C.: Langara College. 2016.
10. hooks, bell. 1994. *Teaching to Transgress: Education as the Practice of Freedom*. New York: Routledge.
11. Perry, Jade T. 2020. "Embodied Sensual Ritual Gems | Grounding Statements." Jade T. Perry. November 15, 2020. https://www.jadetperry.com/blog/embodied-sensual-ritual-gems-grounding-statements.

INDEX